Books by David D. Wilson

A Study on the Holy Ghost
A Study on the Three Johns
The Revelation of Jesus Christ
A Study on the Warnings of Jude
A Study on the Two Peters

Order your copy at:

www.ParadiseGospelPress.com

or contact us at

Paradise Gospel Press
P.O. Box 184
Paradise, Texas 76073

A Study on the Warnings of Jude

Rev. David D. Wilson

A STUDY ON THE WARNINGS OF JUDE,
Wilson, David D.

First Edition

PARADISE GOSPEL PRESS

www.paradisegospelpress.com

This book may not be reproduced in whole or in part, by electronic process or any other means, without permission of the author.

ISBN: 978-1-946823-03-8

Copyright © 2018 by David D. Wilson

All Rights Reserved

Dedication

I would like to dedicate this book to those who have supported me in my journey of writing and publishing the books that God has led me to complete.

First, my wife, Cynthia, for her support, encouragement and her help with deciphering my handwriting as well as my grammar.

Second, my brother-in-law, Farley Dunn of Three Skillet Publishing, for his encouragement, help, and walking me through the process to get to this point. Mr. Dunn was very instrumental in helping me get to the point of wanting my works published and remains a big help. Thank you again for all your help, Farley, because without you there would not be as many books as there are.

Finally, yet importantly, I want to thank my children and grandchildren for their understanding, encouragement and even giving me hints of which studies they wanted me to do next.

Jude

A Jewel in 25 Verses

Table of Contents

A Jewel in 25 Verses	......	11
Review Questions	......	15
A General Epistle	......	17
Review Questions	......	19
Verses 1-2	......	21
Review Questions	......	33
Verse 3	......	35
Review Questions	......	41
Verse 4	......	43
Review Questions	......	51
Verse 5	......	53
Review Questions	......	61
Verse 6	......	63
Review Questions	......	71
Verse 7	......	73
Review Questions	......	85
Verse 8	......	87
Review Questions	......	91
Verse 9	......	93
Review Questions	......	97
Verse 10	......	99
Review Questions	......	103
Verse 11	......	105
Review Questions	......	115
Verses 12-13	......	117
Review Questions	......	123
Verses 14-16	......	125
Review Questions	......	129
Verses 17-19	......	131
Review Questions	......	135
Verses 20-21	......	137
Review Questions	......	141

Verses 22-25 143
Review Questions 147

Bibliography

Answers

Introduction

Jude

A Jewel in 25 Verses

The book of Jude is a small book; it has only twenty-five verses. But these twenty-five verses are very important to the Christian believer. This book is a warning to the Christian Church and believers. Sadly, Jude goes unnoticed and unread. In one of the revivals our church was in, the evangelist preached every night for two weeks. I still preached the Sunday morning services. One of those Sunday mornings the Lord led me to preach out of the book of Jude. After the service was over the evangelist came up to me and said these words: "You know, I didn't know all of that was in Jude."
Just because a book is small doesn't mean that it's

Note: In this study, all scripture is quoted from the *King James Version* unless otherwise stated. All scriptures are italicized.

unimportant. Remember, all scripture is given by the inspiration of God, thus there is something that is important in every book and chapter in the Bible. Jude is extremely important because of the warnings that God lays before us in these verses. The warnings deal with the way we live and the things we do. It also deals with **warnings against corrupt preachers, teachers and ungodly heresies.** Heresies are teachings that pervert the true Word of God.

An example is the teaching that Jesus, God's only begotten Son, and the devil are brothers. That we are God's spirit children, and that we left heaven to be born on earth like Jesus. This teaching says that Jesus and the devil are brothers, and we are the brothers and sisters of both Jesus and the devil. This philosophy is an outright lie. We are the children of God, but **only through the shed blood of Jesus Christ**; we are the children of God by adoption, when we accept Jesus as our Savior. The devil is not the brother of our Lord Jesus, neither is the devil our brother. This is just one example; there are thousands more.

Jude stresses that we must be aware, and we must be knowledgeable of the true Word of God. **The lack of knowledge is one of the most fatal mistakes Christians can make.** We must teach the pure Word of God, because today's church world is teaching a very perverted gospel. The closer we get to the return of our Lord, the further away from God the church seems to try and get. Preachers offer their reasons for their actions, but I am persuaded that God has had enough. **Preach the truth or suffer for our actions.**

Remember, no one lives to themselves; **everything we do affects those we love and those around us.** Whether people will admit it or not, the things we say, the actions we put forth, affect the lives of loved ones and those we consider friends. Take a drunkard. His or her actions affect his or her spouse and children, if there are any. Drinking has caused many a marriage to come to an end. Unfaithfulness has caused many to leave their spouse and go their separate ways. **Your actions and attitudes cause reactions and attitudes, believe it or not.**

In church, **actions either cause people to praise and worship God, or, in many cases, turn people off towards God.** Many a time I have heard different people say, well if that's being a Christian, I want nothing to do with it. The central and most important goal of the church and believers is to win lost souls for our Lord and Savior Jesus Christ, the only begotten Son of our Almighty God and Father. I hope this Bible study will open eyes to where people stand with God. Whether you study Jude alone or in a group, I have tried to make this study simple to understand, yet to bring out the full meanings of the warnings given to the Christian believer who studies and searches the scriptures, for in them, there is hope, life, and comfort to the believers.

Review of A Jewel in 25 Verses

1. How many verses are in Jude?

   _____

2. This book is what to Christian churches and believers?

   _____

   _____

3. What are heresies?

   _____

   _____

   _____

4. What makes us the children of God?

   _____

   _____

   _____

5. What is one of the most fatal mistakes Christians can make?

   _____

   _____

6. What is the most important goal of the church?

   _____

   _____

   _____

A General Epistle

The book of Jude is what is referred to as a general epistle. This means that it is not directed to any person or group in particular. Most of the epistles are directed to particular people such as Timothy or to churches such as the churches of Galatia. **Jude is, however, directed to all Christians everywhere.** Thus, it is called general.

This epistle is to the new-found church in Jesus Christ; its message is to every Christian whether they came out of paganism or out of the Jewish faith. This epistle is and always will be of great value to Christians and Christian churches. It is very much like parts of II Peter. Jude is a warning to us that we must ever be vigilant, for there are in the world many seducers, who are leading weak and unstable Christians away from the presence of God. **These seducers have a form of godliness but deny the power thereof**, and scripture tells us to turn away from these seducers and seductions that would damn our souls to a devil's hell.

Just as there are warnings, Jude also inspires us to

seek after godly things in Christ Jesus, that through our love for and in Jesus we might gain spiritual strength and a closer walk with the Master. **One of the great dangers in the church today is indifference.** We've heard the gospel message so many times that we've come to the place that the gospel no longer has that special place of importance in our lives. Remember Lot who dwelt in the cities of the plain? Scripture tells us that his soul was vexed by the evil around him. A modern example would be that when we work in a place where we are around sinners all the time, at first their cursing really bothers us, but as time goes by, we become accustomed to it, and then think nothing of it. We then become like Lot. **Without a constant prayer life, we fall prey to the wiles of the devil.** If we as God's servants slumber and sleep, the enemy will come and sow tares in our fields. **We must ever be watchful.**

Review of A General Epistle

1. What kind of epistle is the book of Jude?

   _____

   _____

2. Why is Jude called a general epistle?

   _____

   _____

   _____

3. Jude is very much like what other book?

   _____

4. What is one of the great dangers in the church today?

   _____

   _____

   _____

5. Why must we have a constant prayer life?

   _____

   _____

   _____

6. What happens when we slumber and sleep?

   _____

   _____

   _____

7. What must we ever be?

   _____

   _____

Jude

Verses 1-2

Jude 1:1-2

¹ Jude, the servant of Jesus Christ, and brother of James, to them that are sanctified by God the Father, and preserved in Jesus Christ, and called: ² Mercy unto you, and peace, and love, be multiplied.

Who is this Jude? Jude, Judas, or Judah, as he has been called, states that he is a servant of Jesus Christ. He also states that he is the brother of James (the Just) and the brother of Jesus.

Matthew 13:53-58

⁵³ And it came to pass, that when Jesus had finished these parables, he departed thence.
⁵⁴ And when he was come into his own country, he taught them in their synagogue, insomuch that they were astonished, and said, Whence hath this man this wisdom, and these mighty works?
⁵⁵ Is not this the carpenter's son? is not his mother called Mary? and his brethren, James, and Joses, and Simon, and Judas?
⁵⁶ And his sisters, are they not all with us? Whence then hath this man all these things?
⁵⁷ And they were offended in him. But Jesus said unto them, A prophet is not without honour, save in his own country, and in his own house.
⁵⁸ And he did not many mighty works there because of their unbelief.

In Matthew 13:55, the brothers of Jesus are named; they are James, Joses, Simon, and Judas.

Mark 6:1-6

¹ And he went out from thence, and came into his own country; and his disciples follow him.
² And when the sabbath day was come, he began to teach in the synagogue: and many hearing him were astonished, saying, From whence hath this man these things? and what wisdom is this which is given unto him, that even such mighty works are wrought by his

hands?
³ Is not this the carpenter, the son of Mary, the brother of James, and Joses, and of Juda, and Simon? and are not his sisters here with us? And they were offended at him.
⁴ But Jesus said unto them, A prophet is not without honour, but in his own country, and among his own kin, and in his own house.
⁵ And he could there do no mighty work, save that he laid his hands upon a few sick folk, and healed them.
⁶ And he marvelled because of their unbelief. And he went round about the villages, teaching.

Here in Mark 6:3, again the brothers of Jesus are named, and they are James, Joses, Juda, and Simon. The scriptures also state that Jesus had sisters. Their names are not given, nor the number of them, but by simple deduction we know that there were at the least two, because scripture states sisters. So, Jude was the brother of Jesus, our Lord.

In this epistle Jude doesn't claim importance as being the brother to Jesus, but with humbleness in his heart, **his only claim is that he is the servant of Jesus Christ.** I can understand the feeling that he must have had that he was not worthy to be called the brother of Jesus, and that his only desire was, **"Just let me be your servant, Lord."**

I believe as Jude was beginning to write this epistle, his mind went back to the days of his youth; the days also when Jesus began his ministry; the day when he and his brothers and sisters refused to believe that Jesus was the promised Messiah. Jesus even spoke of it in Mark.

Mark 6:4

> *But Jesus said unto them, A prophet is not without honour, but in his own country, and among his own kin, and in his own house.*

Here Jesus admits that his family refused to believe in Him. They refused to accept Jesus because they, like all Israel, were looking for a great warrior king, a king who would come and once again make Israel a great nation. That wasn't the will of God for that time, though it will come in the future when Jesus returns. When did Jude repent and receive salvation? When did Jude accept Jesus as the promised Lord and Savior, the Messiah? We don't know.

The scripture does record that Jesus appeared to James after the resurrection. (I Corinthians 15:5-7) So it was shortly after this event, because the scripture tells us so. As we study the scripture, we find that Mary, the mother of Jesus, and Jesus' brothers were among the one hundred and twenty praying in the upper room when the Holy Ghost was poured out on the day of Pentecost.

Acts 1:13-14

> *[13] And when they were come in, they went up into an upper room, where abode both Peter, and James, and John, and Andrew, Philip, and Thomas, Bartholomew, and Matthew, James the son of Alphaeus, and Simon Zelotes, and Judas the brother of James.*
> *[14] These all continued with one accord in prayer and supplication, with the women, and Mary the mother*

of Jesus, and with his brethren.

Jude does claim to be the brother of James. Some think this was to give his epistle more authority, since James was the head of the church in Jerusalem. Jude, like many of the other apostles, worked in the background, where Paul, Peter, and others worked in the foreground. **Jude did not seek self-glory, but only to please the Lord.** For Jesus, himself, tells us that *"he that heareth his word and doeth it, is as his brother, and sister, and mother."*

Matthew 12:47-50

> *47 Then one said unto him, Behold, thy mother and thy brethren stand without, desiring to speak with thee.*
> *48 But he answered and said unto him that told him, Who is my mother? and who are my brethren?*
> *49 And he stretched forth his hand toward his disciples, and said, Behold my mother and my brethren!*
> *50 For whosoever shall do the will of my Father which is in heaven, the same is my brother, and sister, and mother.*

We can have no greater witness than to have it said about us that we were humble servants of our Lord Jesus Christ. Jude directs this epistle: *"to them that are sanctified by God the Father, and preserved in Jesus Christ, and called:"*

Who are the called? The scripture states that many are called but few are chosen.

Matthew 20:16

So the last shall be first, and the first last: for many be called, but few chosen.

Matthew 22:14

For many are called, but few are chosen.

Who are the chosen? The chosen are all those who repent of their sins and accept Jesus Christ as their Savior. God is not willing that any should perish but that all should have everlasting life. You say, "What's the catch?" There is no catch; **the only requirement is that you, of your own free will, repent and accept Jesus as your Savior**. God will not make us do anything against our will; if we make heaven our home, it's because we chose to serve the Lord. If we make hell our home, it's solely because we chose to do so. **God sends no one to hell; we send ourselves there**, because of our own choices, actions, and desires.

I know that there are those who contend that we don't have a choice, but they are wrong. **We are not put upon this earth with no choice as to our final outcome.** Every one of us has the same opportunity; what we make of it is up to our own discretion. The Word tells that many are called, many are bid to the marriage. It is not God's will that any should perish, but that all should be saved. It's up to us; **God will not make a man serve Him.** If God forced us to serve, there would be no love. In the past some men and women were made slaves. Did they like their lives? Did they want to be slaves? The answer is no. They desired to be free to make their own decisions, to be their own person. God gives us this opportunity, the opportunity to decide, but **we will also reap the rewards of those decisions**, be it good or be it bad.

Matthew 22:9

> *Go ye therefore into the highways, and as many as ye shall find, bid to the marriage.*

Romans 10:9-13

> *⁹ That if thou shalt confess with thy mouth the Lord Jesus, and shalt believe in thine heart that God hath raised him from the dead, thou shalt be saved.*
> *¹⁰ For with the heart man believeth unto righteousness; and with the mouth confession is made unto salvation.*
> *¹¹ For the scripture saith, Whosoever believeth on him shall not be ashamed.*
> *¹² For there is no difference between the Jew and the Greek: for the same Lord over all is rich unto all that call upon him.*
> *¹³ For whosoever shall call upon the name of the Lord shall be saved.*

1 Timothy 2:4

> *Who will have all men to be saved, and to come unto the knowledge of the truth.*

Revelation 22:16-17

^{16} I Jesus have sent mine angel to testify unto you these things in the churches. I am the root and the offspring of David, and the bright and morning star.
^{17} And the Spirit and the bride say, Come. And let him that heareth say, Come. And let him that is athirst come. And whosoever will, let him take the water of life freely.

The summons (or call, or invitation) is given; what is your answer? I have heard all manner of reasons why people will not go to church and serve the Lord. The one used most is that the church is full of hypocrites, and I concede that this is true. But **there is a judgment day coming very soon.** So, until that day comes, the wheat and the tares must grow together; just know that the harvest is near.

Matthew 13:24-30

^{24} Another parable put he forth unto them, saying, The kingdom of heaven is likened unto a man which sowed good seed in his field:
^{25} But while men slept, his enemy came and sowed tares among the wheat, and went his way.
^{26} But when the blade was sprung up, and brought forth fruit, then appeared the tares also.
^{27} So the servants of the householder came and said unto him, Sir, didst not thou sow good seed in thy field? from whence then hath it tares?
^{28} He said unto them, An enemy hath done this. The

servants said unto him, Wilt thou then that we go and gather them up?
²⁹ But he said, Nay; lest while ye gather up the tares, ye root up also the wheat with them.
³⁰ Let both grow together until the harvest: and in the time of harvest I will say to the reapers, Gather ye together first the tares, and bind them in bundles to burn them: but gather the wheat into my barn.

The rapture of the saints is coming soon, but what of those who are left? There are those who will propose to live for God regardless of the cost they must pay, and there will be some. After the rapture has taken place, the only way for them to enter heaven is to purpose to give their lives for the sake of God's kingdom. **At the great white throne judgment there will be the final separating.** The tares or sinners will be cast into the fire.

The biggest problem with the churches today is that the door to the world has been opened wide and the devil has walked right on in. The world is dictating what the morals and standards of the church are to be. When you make sinners feel comfortable in the church and there is no condemnation, there is no preaching of the true Word of God. The church has failed. Let's be truthful, **the church has backslidden in favor of man's praise.** The church is used to ease the conscience of ungodly men.

James 3:14-16

¹⁴ But if ye have bitter envying and strife in your hearts, glory not, and lie not against the truth.

> *¹⁵ This wisdom descendeth not from above, but is earthly, sensual, devilish.*
> *¹⁶ For where envying and strife is, there is confusion and every evil work.*

Jude, in this epistle, as we shall see, is **giving a warning to not give heed to the many voices of the enemy.** We are to be established in the Word of God, and not be led astray. James 3:14-16 tells us there should be no bitter envying and strife in our hearts, and that we are not to lie. But preachers and teachers get up and lie to people in every service in most churches today. This is the result of letting the world and governments dictate to the church of the living God what morals and standards are acceptable to them. **Whatever happened to letting God set the rules?** It's a shame that people think they know more about what's morally acceptable than God's Word. James 3:15-16 states, *"This wisdom descendeth not from above, but is earthly, sensual, devilish. For where envying and strife is, there is confusion and every evil work."* There's enough evil in the world without the church being full of bitterness, envy, strife, and confusion, but it's here in our midst. The only way to get rid of it in our churches is to pray it out. Then preach the truth of God's Word. **The truth will set us free.**

John 8:23 says: *"And he said unto them, Ye are from beneath; I am from above: ye are of this world; I am not of this world."* To be sanctified by God is to be set apart from the world by the shed blood of Jesus Christ. We are to give ourselves to the service of Christ Jesus and God the Father, laying aside every weight and sin, and **living in the presence of God through Jesus Christ.** In so doing, we are preserved unto God, and at the end of this life we will enter into the presence of God and into that place that Jesus has prepared for us, as He has promised.

Review Questions
for Verses 1-2

1. Who is this Jude?

   _____

   _____

   _____

2. Did Jesus have any sisters, and if so, how many?

   _____

   _____

   _____

3. Who was the head of the church in Jerusalem?

   _____

   _____

   _____

4. Jude directs this epistle to whom?

   _____

   _____

   _____

5. Does God send souls to hell?

   _____

   _____

   _____

6. Is there a chance to make heaven if we miss the rapture? If so, how?

   _____

   _____

   _____

7. Who is dictating the church's morals today?

   _____

   _____

   _____

8. What will set us free?

   _____

   _____

   _____

Verse 3

Jude 1:3

Beloved, when I gave all diligence to write unto you of the common salvation, it was needful for me to write unto you, and exhort you that ye should earnestly contend for the faith which was once delivered unto the saints.

Jude begins this third verse by saying, *"I gave all diligence to write unto you."* Jude was greatly troubled by what was going on in the churches. **False teachers had arisen to pervert the gospel** to lead men and women into false beliefs and away from the truth of God's Word. Pagan idols had come into the churches, and along with these pagan idols, the teaching of Gnosticism was coming into the churches as well.

In the book *A Summary of Christian History*, it states: "The roots of Gnosticism may be found in Jewish writings like those of Philo of Alexandria (20 BC - 40 AD)." "Gnosticism was a search for salvation through knowledge." "Gnosticism attempted to explain the nature of evil, the nature of God and his relation to the world, and the present order of existence." All of these things were coming against the newly founded churches and new Christian believers. The **devil was trying to destroy the faith of newborn saints**; something had to be done.

When Jude speaks of giving all diligence to writing to the Christians, he is saying he has thought much and prayed much on how to best address the problems that were among them. He then stresses the fact of a common salvation. There was much contention; each faction in the church said their beliefs and their ideas were the right ones. Does this remind you of the church today? Jude's epistle in this third verse is trying to **bring everyone back to the knowledge that we are saved by a common salvation**; common in the fact that we are all saved the very same way.

Salvation comes through the repenting of our sins and the acceptance of salvation through the shed blood of Jesus Christ. Jude was grieved in his heart at what was happening. Paul was also very concerned that the church was suffering from the onslaught of the enemy. Paul wrote to the Galatians, *"I marvel that ye are so soon removed from him that called you into the grace of Christ unto another gospel:"*

Galatians 1:6-10

⁶ *I marvel that ye are so soon removed from him that*

called you into the grace of Christ unto another gospel:

⁷ Which is not another; but there be some that trouble you, and would pervert the gospel of Christ

But though we, or an angel from heaven, preach any other gospel unto you than that which we have preached unto you, let him be accursed.

⁹ As we said before, so say I now again, If any man preach any other gospel unto you than that ye have received, let him be accursed.

¹⁰ For do I now persuade men, or God? or do I seek to please men? for if I yet pleased men, I should not be the servant of Christ.

We must be ever vigilant, praying for wisdom and knowledge to discern the tricks and snares of the devil. As we look around us, we can see how the church world is bending and bowing at the altar of the world. Look at how most churches have changed their church doctrine to go directly opposite of the true Word of God; how they've tried to rewrite the Bible to say what they want it to say. I, like Paul, Jude, and others, marvel at **how quickly men are turning the truth of God's Word into a lie.**

Jude goes on to stress that we *"should earnestly contend for the faith which was once delivered unto the saints."* Jesus came to seek and save that which was lost. **Our Lord made no distinction between Jew and Gentile when they were moved by faith.** The New Testament tells us that in Christ Jesus, there is neither Jew nor Greek.

Mark 16:15-16

^{15} And he said unto them, Go ye into all the world, and preach the gospel to every creature.
^{16} He that believeth and is baptized shall be saved; but he that believeth not shall be damned.

Jesus in these scriptures said: *"Go ye into all the world, and preach the gospel to every creature."* This speaks of the common salvation. **All that it takes is to repent and believe.** Salvation is to everyone, like the children's song: *red and yellow, black and white; they are precious in his sight.* Jew or pagan, it makes no difference. **This common salvation is for everyone.**

Romans 1:16

For I am not ashamed of the gospel of Christ: for it is the power of God unto salvation to every one that believeth; to the Jew first, and also to the Greek.

This verse speaks volumes; *"the power of God unto salvation."* Who can save the soul blackened by sin? No one but Jesus. Who can change hearts? No one but Jesus. What can make us whole again? Nothing but the blood of Jesus. The next part of that verse says, *"to every one that believeth, to the Jew first and also to the Greek."* There is no doubt, this salvation is a common salvation, that everyone must come to Jesus the same, even the Jews. **There are no short cuts, no special privileges**; we all come the same way.

The last part speaks of the gift of salvation that was

delivered to the saints. It is ours, but we must earnestly contend, strive, fight for, hold onto, that it not slip away. Pray earnestly and hold fast, that no man take thy crown. The preaching of the gospel is the only way that this salvation can be delivered. When I speak of the preaching of the gospel, ninety percent of people instantly think of preachers behind pulpits, but **we preach or deliver the gospel by witnessing to friends and family members, knocking on doors, inviting people to church, and talking to them about the Lord and about their souls.** So the next time you say, "But I'm not a preacher," maybe you are; because **everyone who spreads the Word by witnessing, by songs or preaching of the Word is delivering salvation to everyone who will accept it**; and those who accept this salvation become "the saints of God."

Review Questions
for Verse 3

1. Why was Jude greatly troubled?

   _____

   _____

   _____

2. What is Gnosticism?

   _____

   _____

   _____

3. What is the common salvation?

   _____

   _____

   _____

4. How has the church changed?

   _____

   _____

5. What was once earnestly delivered to the saints?

_____

_____

_____

6. Who are we to preach the gospel to?

_____

_____

_____

7. What is the only way that salvation can be delivered?

_____

_____

_____

Verse 4

Jude 1:4

For there are certain men crept in unawares, who were before of old ordained to this condemnation, ungodly men, turning the grace of our God into lasciviousness, and denying the only Lord God, and our Lord Jesus Christ.

This fourth verse is a **warning to every church and pastor that the devil is out to destroy us**, and if he can't do it from the outside, he will try to do it from the inside. The verse begins, *"For there are certain men crept in unawares."* Who are these men, and what is their purpose? It is to destroy the church of Jesus Christ. These people, be they man or woman, come into our midst putting forth a show of holiness and godly living, but it's all a lie. It has never been more important to Christians than it is today: we must know the Word. **We must teach and preach the truth of God's**

Word. For one day, in the near future, we will stand and give an accounting for all we have said and done.

If we are to hold our Christian brothers and sisters in the truth, we must teach them *"thus sayeth the Word of the Lord."* I don't believe that we, as pastors and teachers, should be dictators or tyrants forcing those around us to bend to our wills. **God does not force us to serve him**, and we should not try to force others to serve God. **The only way to serve God is by our free will and desire to do so.** But, there are many today who come in, and their only desire is to "water down," to weaken the truth of God's Word, to pervert the truth a little here and a little there until the truth is no longer recognized.

I was at a church meeting some time ago and met a minister there who told me that he had heard me preach before. He said that I had done a good job of bringing the Word, but he felt that I had preached too strong a message and should have weakened it down. This is the point that I'm trying to bring out. This is the problem in the churches today. **The world does not want anybody to tell them that they are wrong.** Their attitude is, "Don't tell me I'm a sinner; don't tell me I'm going to hell; I don't want to hear it."

I heard a woman say, "I'm a sinner. I'm supposed to sin, and when Jesus died on the cross, he died to cover my sins when I die." What kind of gospel is being preached and taught in our churches? A perverted gospel that has no power to save. It's only a form of godliness that has no power and will not save.

2 Timothy 3:1-5

> *¹ This know also, that in the last days perilous times shall come.*
> *² For men shall be lovers of their own selves, covetous, boasters, proud, blasphemers, disobedient to parents, unthankful, unholy,*
> *³ Without natural affection, trucebreakers, false accusers, incontinent, fierce, despisers of those that are good,*
> *⁴ Traitors, heady, highminded, lovers of pleasures more than lovers of God;*
> *⁵ Having a form of godliness, but denying the power thereof: from such turn away.*

Jude plainly sees the problems that the devil is throwing at the church. **The devil couldn't stamp out this Christian movement by persecution and killing the saints.** That only spread the word more; he had to find another way. So he went back to his tried and tested forms of deception.

2 Peter 2:1-3

> *¹ But there were false prophets also among the people, even as there shall be false teachers among you, who privily shall bring in damnable heresies, even denying the Lord that bought them, and bring upon themselves swift destruction.*
> *² And many shall follow their pernicious ways; by reason of whom the way of truth shall be evil spoken of.*
> *³ And through covetousness shall they with feigned*

words make merchandise of you: whose judgment now of a long time lingereth not, and their damnation slumbereth not.

Solomon made the statement that there is nothing new under the sun, and how true that is. **We should not be surprised at what the devil is doing to destroy the church.** How many different versions of the Bible do we have today, each one different in certain ways from the others? This is simply another way that the devil has crept in unawares. We must try the spirits to see if they are of God. We must be **close enough to God that we have the "discerning of spirits,"** so that we know who is true and who is false.

The next part of the fourth verse speaks of *"who were before of old ordained to this condemnation, ungodly men."* This does not mean that these particular men and women were picked to do what they are doing by God. They are spoken of in the Old Testament. **The true prophets of God condemned the false prophet.** There have always been those who are out for self only. Deceitful men who prey upon others, they boast of themselves to gain followers, instead of praising God and giving God the glory. These ungodly men and women lead astray those who are not rooted in the Word. But as we said before, these men were not picked to do what they are doing. They have, like others before them, been led away from God by the tricks of the enemy.

The condemnation that is spoken of here is the judgment of sinners before God. All men are ordained to be saved. Jesus' blood was shed for the sins of all mankind. The price has been paid. **We must make the decision as to**

where we will spend eternity. From the foundation of the world, mankind has had only one of two places to spend eternity as ordained of God, heaven or hell. **We and only we make the decision** where we will go.

The ungodly men in this fourth verse are like all ungodly men. Their lives are ruled by pleasure, greed, and by self-esteem. They take the Word of God, only the parts that best suit their plans. They reject and try to do away with the rest. You can say that all ungodly men are the same. Here I would disagree with you. These men spoken of in this fourth verse are using God and God's people to further their own ends.

2 Peter 2:3

And through covetousness shall they with feigned words make merchandise of you: whose judgment now of a long time lingereth not, and their damnation slumbereth not.

All sin is ordained to be punished, and all men have sinned and come short of the glory of God. Though **all have sinned, there is a difference between the Christian and the sinner.** The sinner's sins follow after them to the judgment, but the Christians, the saints of God, their sins have gone on before them; because **as we repent of our sins, they are forgiven, and they do not follow after us.** They have already gone before God.

The devil's crowd denies God's power. They deny the very existence of God. They say there is no God; we accept them as lost, ungodly, and unsaved as sinners. But the other crowd that follows Satan, those who have crept into the church, are far worse. Little by little they nibble away at the truth of God's Word, changing it to say what the world wants. Example: the Bible, the true Word of God, condemns homosexuality. But the politically correct, those that bow before the altar of the world, say that it's OK, that God made them that way. WRONG. God made Adam and Eve. He did not make Adam and Steve. He did not make Eve and Jane. **God does not make mistakes.** The devil takes what God has made and tries to bend, change, and conform it into something else. By small changes, the enemy tries to destroy the souls of man.

Another example of how a small change condemns souls is this: You must be saved, born again, and join the church. Then in a second breath, we're told that you must sin every day. So, the question is: Are you saved from sin and on your way to heaven, or are you a sinner who sins every day and on your way to hell? **My answer to this question is this: I once was a sinner, but now I am saved by grace.** We must be very careful and very sensitive to the Word and how people use it. Little changes can change the true meaning of God's Word.

One version of the Bible speaks of the Virgin Mary as a young woman named Mary. When you change Mary from a virgin to a young woman, you do away with the deity of Christ; you do away with the miracle birth. You do away with Jesus being the Son of God and our promised Savior. Small changes do great harm; be very, very careful. **If it doesn't come out of the Bible, don't believe it.**

When the pastor, preacher, or teacher reads the Word, follow along with them in your Bible; be sure what they are reading is the same as your Bible. **Take no one at their word when it comes to God's Word; your soul is at stake.**

Review Questions
for Verse 4

1. This fourth verse is what?

   _____

   _____

   _____

2. What is the purpose of those who creep in unawares?

   _____

   _____

   _____

3. What is the only way to serve God?

   _____

   _____

   _____

4. Solomon made what statement?

   _____

   _____

   _____

5. Who makes the decision where we will spend eternity?

   _____

   _____

6. What is the difference between the sinners and the saints of God?

   _____

   _____

   _____

7. I once was a sinner but now I am?

   _____

   _____

8. Small changes can do what?

   _____

   _____

   _____

Verse 5

Jude 1:5

I will therefore put you in remembrance, though ye once knew this, how that the Lord, having saved the people out of the land of Egypt, afterward destroyed them that believed not.

The book of Jude again is very much like the second chapter of the Book of II Peter. It carries a dire warning about trusting in the arm of flesh and not in God's love and keeping power. As we look at this fifth verse, **we see Jude seeking to remind the church of where they came from and where they are going.** Jude writes that his desire was to put the church in remembrance of things they already knew. We know many things; our heads are full of the things we've learned through years of experience, but **sometimes we need to be reminded again of what those things are.** Our knowledge is stored in our minds, but much of that knowledge is set aside; in a way, it only comes to the forefront when it is needed. Again, this knowledge is brought to the forefront when we are **reminded of it through someone or something that takes place around us.** When we go to church, we go to learn God's Word and to be reminded of what we have already learned as we read and study our Bibles. We, as ministers and teachers, preach and teach thus sayeth the Word of God. When we were in school, as some are now, we learned much by repetition, going over and over the same material until it was ingrained into our minds. Like spelling, we write the spelling words over and over until we know how to spell them.

The minister, the pastor of a flock, essentially is doing the same thing. **By the preaching of God's Word, the minister is bringing it to remembrance or refreshing our minds on what we know already.** In the case of new Christians, the minister is teaching them God's Word. This is why it's so important for Christians to attend church services on a regular basis, **to have our minds and hearts continually stirred, and to think on godly things.**

2 Peter 3:1-2

> *¹ This second epistle, beloved, I now write unto you; in both which I stir up your pure minds by way of remembrance: ² That ye may be mindful of the words which were spoken before by the holy prophets, and of the commandment of us the apostles of the Lord and Saviour:*

Peter wrote in this first verse that his goal was to "*stir up your pure minds by way of remembrance."* The mind is a very complex organ. If we could unlock its depths, we could remember everything that we have ever learned, heard, or experienced. This, unfortunately, cannot be done in this day and hour. So, **the things we hear and experience on a daily basis are the things we remember the most.** They are the easiest to recall.

In the second verse Peter exhorts us to *"be mindful of the words which were spoken before,"* the words of the prophets and the commandments of the apostles.

Jude, like Peter, **uses illustrations to bring the people's minds back to what God has done** and what God will do if we whole-heartily trust and serve Him. The first example Jude gives is Israel. Israel was in bondage in Egypt; they were little more than slaves. God heard their cries and provided a savior; his name was Moses. Through Moses' obedience to God, the children of Israel were set free.

Keep in mind that **not everyone who left Egypt really wanted to go.** Then why, you say, didn't they just stay in Egypt? Because **they were afraid to stay.** God had just killed every first-born child, as well as the first born of the animals. Egypt was in shock, and everyone that stayed would surely have been killed. So, everyone left. This is why Moses had so much trouble with part of the people. After their long journey, they came to the river of Jordan. The Promised Land was just on the other side. Did they march across and take the land that was promised to them? No. Again, they were afraid, even after God delivered them from Pharaoh's army, gave them manna and meat to eat and gave them water where there was no water. Still, they were afraid; they sent in the twelve spies to spy out the land and give a report.

Ten men said they couldn't conquer the land, and only two trusted God. **Because of their unbelief, every person who was twenty years old and up would die.** They would never set foot in the Promised Land. The only two exceptions were Joshua and Caleb, the two spies who believed God. These two men believed that God would go before them, and that through God, they would well be able to take the Promised Land. **Because of unbelief, the Israelites were condemned to wonder in the wilderness** until all who were condemned died.

They wondered for forty years. Forty years wasted, forty years they could have enjoyed the Promised Land, if only they had trusted God. Saints, **if we will put our trust in God, have faith and believe, we will truly be surprised at what God will do for those that love Him and serve Him.**

This is the first example.

Remember Paul who said: *"Ye did run well; who did hinder you that ye should not obey the truth?"* (Galatians 5:7) **Everything always comes back to obeying the truth, knowing in whom we believe, having faith in God when no help is in sight**, but knowing within ourselves that God is able. Be like the three Hebrew children before the king.

Daniel 3:16-18

> *[16] Shadrach, Meshach, and Abednego, answered and said to the king, O Nebuchadnezzar, we are not careful to answer thee in this matter.*
> *[17] If it be so, our God whom we serve is able to deliver*

us from the burning fiery furnace, and he will deliver us out of thine hand, O king.
¹⁸ But if not, be it known unto thee, O king, that we will not serve thy gods, nor worship the golden image which thou hast set up.

We must stand and be strong, for **we stand not in our own power but in the power of a living God.** When we lose our faith in God and His true Word, we become prey for every trick of the enemy and are easily led astray into unbelief.

Let's read what Paul had to say.

1 Corinthians 10:1-12

¹ Moreover, brethren, I would not that ye should be ignorant, how that all our fathers were under the cloud, and all passed through the sea;
² And were all baptized unto Moses in the cloud and in the sea;
³ And did all eat the same spiritual meat;
⁴ And did all drink the same spiritual drink: for they drank of that spiritual Rock that followed them: and that Rock was Christ.
⁵ But with many of them God was not well pleased: for they were overthrown in the wilderness.
⁶ Now these things were our examples, to the intent we should not lust after evil things, as they also lusted.
⁷ Neither be ye idolaters, as were some of them; as it is written, The people sat down to eat and drink, and

rose up to play.
⁸ Neither let us commit fornication, as some of them committed, and fell in one day three and twenty thousand.
⁹ Neither let us tempt Christ, as some of them also tempted, and were destroyed of serpents.
¹⁰ Neither murmur ye, as some of them also murmured, and were destroyed of the destroyer.
¹¹ Now all these things happened unto them for ensamples: and they are written for our admonition, upon whom the ends of the world are come.
¹² Wherefore let him that thinketh he standeth take heed lest he fall.

As we read these scriptures, we again see that Paul is doing the same thing that Jude is doing. **Paul is trying to stir the minds and hearts of the Corinthian church and to bring to the people's remembrance what God had done** for the Israelites from the time they left Egypt. **Unbelief separates us from God.** Unbelief leads us to live ungodly lives, and **sin destroys us and our relationship with God.**

Romans 11:20-21

²⁰ Well; because of unbelief they were broken off, and thou standest by faith. Be not highminded, but fear:
²¹ For if God spared not the natural branches, take heed lest he also spare not thee.

In Romans 11:20-21, we again hear a warning given

by Paul to the Romans. God's Word is full of warnings. We must take heed. Matthew Henry states of the Israelites: "They had miracles in abundance and they were their daily bread; yet even they perished in unbelief. We have greater (much greater) advantages than they had; let their error (their fatal error) be our awful warning." In closing our comments on this fifth verse, we again look to what Paul had to say: *"For whosoever shall call upon the name of the Lord shall be saved."* (Romans 10:13) Paul's words give us hope, encouragement, and assurance that **if we put our faith in God, God will not let us down.** No matter how hard the trial or how bad the temptation, **God will always make a way of escape for His saints.**

Review Questions
for Verse 5

1. Jude writes that his desire was to put the church in what?_____

   _____

   _____

2. How do we learn?

   _____

   _____

   _____

3. Paul wrote that his goal was to?

   _____

   _____

   _____

4. What is Jude's first illustration?

   _____

   _____

   _____

5. Because of Israel's unbelief, who was condemned to die?

   _____

   _____

6. How long did Israel wander in the wilderness?

   _____

   _____

7. God will always make what for His saints?

   _____

   _____

Verse 6

Jude 1:6

And the angels which kept not their first estate, but left their own habitation, he hath reserved in everlasting chains under darkness unto the judgment of the great day.

    Jude in this verse gives us another example to stir our minds and hearts, to bring to our remembrance what we already know and sadly seem to have forgotten. It is so easy to get caught up in the everyday cares of life and to let certain things slide for the moment. Our problem is that **the things we let slide too often are the most important: our belief and trust in God.** We attend church services, but when we get home, God is put on the back burner. Big mistake. If God isn't first in our lives, He won't be second or third. **If God isn't first, He won't be at all.** The main point that Jude is trying to get over to us is that God will and does hold us accountable for our unbelief, our actions, and the choices we make. To make this point as strong as possible, Jude draws our attention to the fallen angels. These angels were persuaded by Satan to rebel against God. Satan led them in a rebellion in which they lost and were cast out of heaven. Jude speaks of them as having *"kept not their first estate, but left their own habitation."*

What do you know about the fallen angels? Sadly, many Christians really have little knowledge about where Satan came from and about his followers, the fallen angels. To get a good understanding of what Jude is trying to say, we need to go back and look at what happened in heaven and at what caused the angels to fall. Now is a good time to ask you a question that I was asked and have asked many others. **Do angels have free will? I maintain that yes, they do, to a certain degree.** If not, how could they have rebelled against God? Let's look at what the Bible says about these fallen angels.

Isaiah 14:12-15

> *¹² How art thou fallen from heaven, O Lucifer, son of the morning! how art thou cut down to the ground, which didst weaken the nations!*
> *¹³ For thou hast said in thine heart, I will ascend into heaven, I will exalt my throne above the stars of God: I will sit also upon the mount of the congregation, in the sides of the north:*
> *¹⁴ I will ascend above the heights of the clouds; I will be like the most High. ¹⁵ Yet thou shalt be brought down to hell, to the sides of the pit.*

In Isaiah 14:12-15, we read about Lucifer, who was called the *"son of the morning,"* some say the morning star. Lucifer, for some reason, became very dissatisfied with his position. **Self-pride and visions of grandeur caused Lucifer to begin to lust in his own mind** and to elevate himself to be equal with God. Little by little, Lucifer began to put his plan into action. You see, when we seek to deceive and to promote ourselves over others, we plan and scheme until the time that we believe all is ready. Then we begin to move to accomplish our desire. We don't know how long Lucifer worked on the angels to get one third of them to follow him. It really doesn't matter.

Ezekiel 28:12-17

> *¹² Son of man, take up a lamentation upon the king of Tyrus, and say unto him, Thus saith the Lord GOD; Thou sealest up the sum, full of wisdom, and perfect in beauty.*
> *¹³ Thou hast been in Eden the garden of God; every precious stone was thy covering, the sardius, topaz, and the diamond, the beryl, the onyx, and the jasper, the sapphire, the emerald, and the carbuncle, and gold: the workmanship of thy tabrets and of thy pipes was prepared in thee in the day that thou wast created.*
> *¹⁴ Thou art the anointed cherub that covereth; and I have set thee so: thou wast upon the holy mountain of God; thou hast walked up and down in the midst of the stones of fire.*
> *¹⁵ Thou wast perfect in thy ways from the day that*

thou wast created, till iniquity was found in thee.
¹⁶ By the multitude of thy merchandise they have filled the midst of thee with violence, and thou hast sinned: therefore I will cast thee as profane out of the mountain of God: and I will destroy thee, O covering cherub, from the midst of the stones of fire.
¹⁷ Thine heart was lifted up because of thy beauty, thou hast corrupted thy wisdom by reason of thy brightness: I will cast thee to the ground, I will lay thee before kings, that they may behold thee.

In Ezekiel 28:12-17, we read that Lucifer is called *"the anointed cherub."* If we look around us today, we see people who think they are better than everybody else. They look better, they dress better, and they know more than everybody else. They are so full of self, that self is all they can see. This must have been the state of mind Lucifer was in, and still is, even today. **Not satisfied that he destroyed himself, even now he seeks to destroy everyone that he can in revenge against God.**

Revelation 12:3-4

³ And there appeared another wonder in heaven; and behold a great red dragon, having seven heads and ten horns, and seven crowns upon his heads.
⁴ And his tail drew the third part of the stars of heaven, and did cast them to the earth: and the dragon stood before the woman which was ready to be delivered, for to devour her child as soon as it was born.

Someone asked me once how I knew how many angels were cast out of heaven. If you read God's Word, you'll be surprised at what you'll learn. This is why the Bible stresses to study God's Word; it serves to bring back to our remembrance things that we already know. In these scriptures, **we not only learn what happened, but also the judgment that was and is to be imposed.**

Revelation 12:3-12

> *³ And there appeared another wonder in heaven; and behold a great red dragon, having seven heads and ten horns, and seven crowns upon his heads.*
> *⁴ And his tail drew the third part of the stars of heaven, and did cast them to the earth: and the dragon stood before the woman which was ready to be delivered, for to devour her child as soon as it was born.*
> *⁵ And she brought forth a man child, who was to rule all nations with a rod of iron: and her child was caught up unto God, and to his throne.*
> *⁶ And the woman fled into the wilderness, where she hath a place prepared of God, that they should feed her there a thousand two hundred and threescore days.*
> *⁷ And there was war in heaven: Michael and his angels fought against the dragon; and the dragon fought and his angels,*
> *⁸ And prevailed not; neither was their place found any more in heaven.*
> *⁹ And the great dragon was cast out, that old serpent,*

called the Devil, and Satan, which deceiveth the whole world: he was cast out into the earth, and his angels were cast out with him.

[10] And I heard a loud voice saying in heaven, Now is come salvation, and strength, and the kingdom of our God, and the power of his Christ: for the accuser of our brethren is cast down, which accused them before our God day and night.

[11] And they overcame him by the blood of the Lamb, and by the word of their testimony; and they loved not their lives unto the death.

[12] Therefore rejoice, ye heavens, and ye that dwell in them. Woe to the inhabiters of the earth and of the sea! for the devil is come down unto you, having great wrath, because he knoweth that he hath but a short time.

In these scriptures, Lucifer is called the great dragon, that old serpent, the Devil and Satan. The devil's angels in verse four are referred to as stars. Thus, we know that a third part of the angels followed after the devil and were cast out of heaven with him. As we study scripture, we know that the devil, full of pride and envy, waged war in heaven against the archangel Michael and his angels. The devil and the angels that were persuaded to follow him lost the war and were cast out of heaven into the earth. **There is no place in heaven for sin, not for angels and not for man.**

2 Peter 2:4

For if God spared not the angels that sinned, but cast

them down to hell, and delivered them into chains of darkness, to be reserved unto judgment;

Peter warns, *"For if God spared not the angels that sinned,"* **how can we think that God will not hold us accountable?** The soul that sinneth, it shall die. As I was studying, I was brought to a new insight. For years I have read about the angels that fell, how they were held in chains of darkness. I've always thought of them in literal chains in a dark place. But God has given me a new insight on this scripture. Angels have always been thought of as beings of light, and in heaven, they are. But perhaps the scripture is not talking about real metal chains. Have you ever been in a deep cave and had the guides turn off the lights? There you stand in the darkest dark you have ever been in. We say when night comes that it's dark outside, but that's not really dark. What greater punishment for angels of light than to be put into total blackness?

I am told that you can never get used to total blackness, such as being in a deep cave, and I can truly believe it. Peter states that these angels are being reserved, or held there, awaiting the final judgment. Jude closes the sixth verse with a similar statement: *"he hath reserved in everlasting chains under darkness unto the judgment of the great day."* Think, **if God spared not his created beings, why we would think that he would spare us if we sin?**

I have heard over and over people say that a loving God would not send or permit a soul to go into a devil's hell. This type of new age teaching is going to cause a lot of people to miss heaven. Heed the warning Jude is giving and **take nothing for granted; your soul is at risk.**

Review Questions
for Verse 6

1. If God is not first in our lives, He will not be what?

   _____

   _____

2. What is the main point that Jude is trying to get over to us? _____

   _____

3. Do angels have free will? _____ Why do you think this?

   _____

   _____

   _____

4. Who did the angel Lucifer become?

   _____

   _____

5. How many angels fell with Lucifer?

   _____

   _____

6. Where are the fallen angels held?

   _____

   _____

Verse 7

Jude 1:7

Even as Sodom and Gomorrha, and the cities about them in like manner, giving themselves over to fornication, and going after strange flesh, are set forth for an example, suffering the vengeance of eternal fire.

In this third example, Jude is trying still to awaken the churches and Christians to the dangers of being led astray by false teachers and ministers. There is an old expression that says if it sounds too good to be true, then it usually is, and you had better leave it alone. When I was first saved, preachers preached a dress code, because the Bible tells us point blank to be modest in apparel. The Bible, as we study it (which most people fail to do), tells us to abstain from the very appearance of evil (*Abstain from all appearance of evil.* 1 Thessalonians 5:22). Fornication will, and has destroyed many a soul; fornication is no respecter of persons. Preachers, teachers and lay members are all subject to temptations. In *Vine's Complete Expository Dictionary of Old and New Testament Words*, it states that fornication is illicit sexual intercourse, and can also include adultery and associating with pagan idolatry. We all know the story of Sodom and Gomorrah, but to those who are not sure, we will look at what the Bible teaches us. First, we go to the book of Genesis.

Genesis 18:20-22

> [20] *And the LORD said, Because the cry of Sodom and Gomorrah is great, and because their sin is very grievous;*
> [21] *I will go down now, and see whether they have done altogether according to the cry of it, which is come unto me; and if not, I will know.*
> [22] *And the men turned their faces from thence, and went toward Sodom: but Abraham stood yet before the LORD.*

The sins of Sodom and Gomorrah were great. The Lord called their sin very grievous. **What made it so grievous? When we turn our backs on what is good and love the things that are evil.** Today people look at the Ten Commandments, and in their minds, they are not commandments from God. To the world and a large part of the church, these are ten suggestions, not commandments.

Their minds don't seem to be able to understand what the word commandment means. **A command is something to be obeyed.** The military officers give commands to the soldiers and expect them to be obeyed. If they are not obeyed, then the soldier or soldiers will be held accountable for their actions, and at times dire punishment will be given out. **We must learn that we are held accountable for our deeds.** For Sodom and Gomorrah, the punishment was total destruction, but not only for Sodom and Gomorrah. The cities of Admah and Zeboim which followed after the same lifestyle suffered the same punishment.

Deuteronomy 29:23-27

> *^{23} And that the whole land thereof is brimstone, and salt, and burning, that it is not sown, nor beareth, nor any grass groweth therein, like the overthrow of Sodom, and Gomorrah, Admah, and Zeboim, which the LORD overthrew in his anger, and in his wrath:*
> *^{24} Even all nations shall say, Wherefore hath the LORD done thus unto this land? what meaneth the heat of this great anger?*
> *^{25} Then men shall say, Because they have forsaken the covenant of the LORD God of their fathers, which he made with them when he brought them forth out of the land of Egypt:*
> *^{26} For they went and served other gods, and worshipped them, gods whom they knew not, and whom he had not given unto them: ^{27} And the anger of the LORD was kindled against this land, to bring upon it all the curses that are written in this book:*

In Deuteronomy, starting with the twenty-ninth chapter, we find more details. Sodom and Gomorrah were built on the well-watered plains where there was good grass and good land for raising food. These cities had everything they needed. They grew rich, but in growing rich, like many nations, they became pleasure mad. The more pleasure they had, the more they wanted. **The more they got, the more evil they became.** The word sodomy is a reflection of the lifestyle these people lived.

What does the world and even a large part of the church say today? I have heard many say, "Well, remember, that was in the Old Testament. We're not living under the law anymore. Today, we're living under grace. Jesus died on the cross for our sins. All I have to do is accept Jesus as my Savior, and I'm OK. After that, it doesn't matter what we do. I believe that Jesus died for my sins."

When we study scripture, we read that at the point of salvation, all our sins are washed away (some say covered by the blood). Scripture also says old things are passed away; behold: all things are made new. **After salvation, if we continue to sin, then our salvation had availed nothing; and if we continue to sin, there is no salvation.**

Jude is sounding out the warning, but who is listening? For those who always try to say, "but that happened in the old Testament," let's look at what Paul had to say on the subject. In Romans, Paul talks about a lifestyle that people were living at that time. It's the same lifestyle that the people of Sodom and Gomorrah were living, and that the world and much of the church is living today.

Romans 1:16-32

^{16} For I am not ashamed of the gospel of Christ: for

it is the power of God unto salvation to every one that believeth; to the Jew first, and also to the Greek.

17 For therein is the righteousness of God revealed from faith to faith: as it is written, The just shall live by faith.

18 For the wrath of God is revealed from heaven against all ungodliness and unrighteousness of men, who hold the truth in unrighteousness;

19 Because that which may be known of God is manifest in them; for God hath shewed it unto them.

20 For the invisible things of him from the creation of the world are clearly seen, being understood by the things that are made, even his eternal power and Godhead; so that they are without excuse:

21 Because that, when they knew God, they glorified him not as God, neither were thankful; but became vain in their imaginations, and their foolish heart was darkened.

22 Professing themselves to be wise, they became fools,

23 And changed the glory of the uncorruptible God into an image made like to corruptible man, and to birds, and fourfooted beasts, and creeping things.

24 Wherefore God also gave them up to uncleanness through the lusts of their own hearts, to dishonour their own bodies between themselves:

25 Who changed the truth of God into a lie, and worshipped and served the creature more than the Creator, who is blessed for ever. Amen.

26 For this cause God gave them up unto vile affections: for even their women did change the natural

use into that which is against nature:
²⁷ And likewise also the men, leaving the natural use of the woman, burned in their lust one toward another; men with men working that which is unseemly, and receiving in themselves that recompence of their error which was meet.
²⁸ And even as they did not like to retain God in their knowledge, God gave them over to a reprobate mind, to do those things which are not convenient;
²⁹ Being filled with all unrighteousness, fornication, wickedness, covetousness, maliciousness; full of envy, murder, debate, deceit, malignity; whisperers,
³⁰ Backbiters, haters of God, despiteful, proud, boasters, inventors of evil things, disobedient to parents,
³¹ Without understanding, covenantbreakers, without natural affection, implacable, unmerciful:
³² Who knowing the judgment of God, that they which commit such things are worthy of death, not only do the same, but have pleasure in them that do them.

Paul begins his discourse with the words, *"For I am not ashamed of the gospel of Christ."* **There are many Christians today who are ashamed of being a Christian** and don't want people to know because of the world's view of Christians. Sadly, some people should be ashamed, for they have no idea what it means to be a child of God. They go to church out of a sense of guilt but never do anything about the guilt they carry. Salvation is free to whosoever will. It is ours; all we have to do is to repent and accept Jesus Christ as our Savior. Then, after we are saved or born again, we must begin to live a life pleasing before the Lord, always remembering that **if we are ashamed of Christ down here, He will be ashamed of us before the Father.**

Mark 8:38

> *Whosoever therefore shall be ashamed of me and of my words in this adulterous and sinful generation; of him also shall the Son of man be ashamed, when he cometh in the glory of his Father with the holy angels.*

Luke 9:26

> *For whosoever shall be ashamed of me and of my words, of him shall the Son of man be ashamed, when he shall come in his own glory, and in his Father's, and of the holy angels.*

I can truly say that I am not ashamed of Christ and of being a Christian, and I surely do not want my Savior to be ashamed of me. **We live by faith and not by sight**, and if Jesus tarries his coming, I am sure things will become more difficult for the church. If I am right and the church comes under persecution, the truly just saints of God will see the unjust fall away. **Come quickly, Lord Jesus.**

Paul goes on to say that the wrath of God is revealed from heaven against the unrighteousness of men. Verse 21 begins, *"Because that, when they knew God, they glorified him not as God."* When the scripture speaks of them knowing God, this says that at one time **they had a relationship with God but let selfish desires lead them away** from the fullness of God.

Next, Paul goes into detail as to how they began to change. We will look at the church world Paul is describing and compare it to the church world today. Paul begins to name their faults. As we list what Paul teaches us about, look closely at the church today; we can see the comparison.

1. They became vain in their imaginations, and their foolish hearts were darkened.
2. Professing themselves to be wise, they became fools.
3. They changed the glory of God, and made images like of corruptible man, birds, four-footed beasts and creeping things.
4. God gave them up to uncleanness through lust, to dishonor their own bodies between themselves.
5. **They changed the truth of God into a lie** and worshipped the creature more than the creator.
6. For this cause God gave them up unto vile affections.
7. Even their women did change the natural use into that which is against nature.
8. Men left the natural use of the woman, burned in their lust one toward another, men with men working that which is unseemly.
9. They did not like to retain God in their knowledge; God gave them over to a reprobate mind.
10. Filled with unrighteousness – (evil intentions)
11. Fornication – (illicit sexual intercourse)
12. Wickedness – (evil)
13. Covetousness – (to desire other's possessions,

positions, relationships, anything that belongs to someone else)
14. Maliciousness – (a vicious character)
15. Full of envy – (to feel jealous of others)
16. Murder – (to take another's life)
17. Debate – (to discuss, to argue in detail)
18. Deceit – (to deceive or defraud)
19. Malignity – (bad character, an evil disposition)
20. Whisperers – (to secretly spread gossip)
21. Backbiters – (those who pretend secrecy to carry out accusations against men)
22. Haters of God – (those who hate everything that has to do with God)
23. Despiteful – (those who act out of spite)
24. Proud – (those who are full of self)
25. Boasters – (to praise oneself extravagantly)
26. Inventors of evil things – (should not need an explanation)
27. Disobedient to parents – (should not need an explanation)
28. Without understanding – (not realizing the results of being held accountable for their actions)
29. Covenant breakers – (not keeping your part of an agreement with man or with God)
30. Without natural affection – (to not have love or compassion for friends or family)
31. Implacable – (one who cannot be appeased or pacified; relentless)
32. Unmerciful – (one who has no mercy; one without natural feeling or compassion)

Romans 1:32

> *Who knowing the judgment of God, that they which commit such things are worthy of death, not only do the same, but have pleasure in them that do them.*

Paul in Romans 1:32 is warning the church that **the aforenamed sins, one or many, will bring God's wrath upon the people who do them.** Peter, in II Peter 2, is giving the same warning. Jude in his writings is giving the same warning to the church, but not so much as to the world. Looking at this list, how many of these things can you see in the church and in the Christians' lives? Sadly we, who walk truly with God, see many of these things in our local congregations. **What is it going to take to wake up the church to the danger they are in?**

1 Peter 4:7, 17-18

> *⁷ But the end of all things is at hand: be ye therefore sober, and watch unto prayer. . . .*
> *¹⁷ For the time is come that judgment must begin at the house of God: and if it first begin at us, what shall the end be of them that obey not the gospel of God?*
> *¹⁸ And if the righteous scarcely be saved, where shall the ungodly and the sinner appear?*

Peter sums up everything in I Peter 4:17 when he states, **"the time is come that judgment must begin at the house of God."** Jude has given three examples of how God will deal with sin. Somehow the church has conceived that because we are now living under grace, everything has changed. We no longer have to live under the rules and laws that God has put in place in the Holy Scriptures. Lying is no longer a sin; homosexuality is no longer a learned sin; God has made mistakes, and people are born that way. We accept men and women into the priesthood (ministry) whose lives do not measure up to scriptural standards set by God. Bible theologians now know more than God, as they would have us to believe. When we let the liberal world dictate moral standards and values to the church of the Living God, we have what we see now, an apostate church that is powerless with God and no good to anyone. **Know what the Word of God says, believe it, stand on it, and live by it;** this is Jude's warning. We cannot go after strange flesh or we risk the vengeance of eternal fire.

Review Questions
for Verse 7

1. What does the Bible tell us to abstain from?

   _____

   _____

2. What is a command?

   _____

   _____

3. What was the punishment of Sodom and Gomorrah?

   _____

   _____

4. Name the two other cities destroyed with Sodom and Gomorrah.

   _____

   _____

5. What happens at Salvation?

   _____

   _____

6. When they changed the truth of God into a lie, they then did what?

   _____

   _____

7. In Romans it tells us that when we do not like to retain God in our knowledge, God does what?

   _____

   _____

8. Scripture states that judgment must begin where?

   _____

   _____

Verse 8

Jude 1:8

Likewise also these filthy dreamers defile the flesh, despise dominion, and speak evil of dignities.

Jude begins this verse talking about filthy dreamers defiling the flesh, be it a daydream or a dream in the night. Jude is trying to show that **all sin starts somewhere in a dream.** These people live in a world of unreality, a world of delusion, a world of fantasy. Here, let me say that not all dreams are sinful. At times God speaks to us in dreams to make us aware of something that we don't know, or to warn us about things to come. This type of dream isn't what Jude is talking about. **He's talking about the birth of sin in our lives,** if we aren't completely committed to God. **Sin starts as a tiny spark and grows** until it begins to occupy the mind and heart of a person. The Bible also calls these sinful dreams delusions.

2 Thessalonians 2:11-12

> *[11] And for this cause God shall send them strong delusion, that they should believe a lie:*
> *[12] That they all might be damned who believed not the truth, but had pleasure in unrighteousness.*

When people believe Satan's lie, then the next step is to turn away from the truth of God's Word. **They believe the lie that Satan told Eve in the garden:** Genesis 3:4-5 . . . *"ye shall be as gods"* . . . Turning from the truth, they feed their minds upon false teachings and man's doctrine, which serves to inflate self.

2 Timothy 4:3-4

> *[3] For the time will come when they will not endure sound doctrine; but after their own lusts shall they heap to themselves teachers, having itching ears;*
> *[4] And they shall turn away their ears from the truth, and shall be turned unto fables.*

They fill themselves with false pride. This only serves to encourage their rebellion against God. **When a person rejects the authority of God's Word, they reject God.** When this happens, that person feels free to live as they desire. With no constraints from God, they turn their lives over to fleshly desires. They live as they please in a world of sin. But there's one thing that they don't consider or think about: **God keeps a record.** When we disobey God's laws, there will come a day when **we face the penalties for what** we've done.

Psalm 73:6-11

> *⁶ Therefore pride compasseth them about as a chain; violence covereth them as a garment.*
> *⁷ Their eyes stand out with fatness: they have more than heart could wish.*
> *⁸ They are corrupt, and speak wickedly concerning oppression: they speak loftily.*
> *⁹ They set their mouth against the heavens, and their tongue walketh through the earth.*
> *¹⁰ Therefore his people return hither: and waters of a full cup are wrung out to them.*
> *¹¹ And they say, How doth God know? and is there knowledge in the most High?*

There are those who today put themselves on the same level as God; the only one that does not make mistakes is God. Man makes mistakes, and he will someday pay for his self-righteous attitudes and rejection of God. **When will we learn that God is the only one who does not make mistakes?**

Yet today we have Bible scholars (countless numbers of them) who think that they are smarter than God, that the Bible is full of mistakes, and that much of the Word doesn't really mean what it says. I heard one Bible scholar say that one example of the Bible being wrong was the feeding of the five thousand with five loaves and two fish. They went on to say that everybody knows that it's impossible to feed five thousand men plus women and children with only the five loaves and two fish. She did agree that Jesus had some sort of power to make sick people feel better. Also, that the people raised from the dead were not really dead; that they were only in some kind of comatose state. This kind of teaching is what's taking place in the church world today. The church world as a whole is being led down the garden path of apostasy, by men and women who think they know more about the Bible, God's Holy Scriptures, than God. And we wonder what has happened to the church, why people no longer hold or live by Christian standards and godly convictions.

It's no wonder that people despise dominion or authority in the church when so-called Bible scholars don't believe the Bible is without error. **The Bible is the true, authoritative Word of God.** Every word is true, every line is true, every verse is true, every chapter is true, every book is true, the whole Bible is true; **to believe otherwise is delusion.** The Bible is the final authority to believe; to do otherwise is a sin against God. Be careful what you say against dignities (those in authority) for **God is in control.** Psalm 105:15 says: *"Saying, Touch not mine anointed, and do my prophets no harm."* **When false teaching is going out about God's Word, and people are being misled, either because of ignorance or personal selfish gain, it's a sin.** What did the word say? *"Touch not mine anointed."* Preachers and teachers, be very careful, for God is keeping a record.

The only hope the world has is in God. The only peace is in God. With God we have what we need to live a happy and contented life. We may not have everything we want in this life, but **with God, we have everything we need.**

Review Questions
for Verse 8

1. Are all dreams sinful?

   _____

   _____

   _____

2. What does the Bible call sinful dreams?

   _____

   _____

   _____

3. What is the lie that Satan told Eve in the garden?

   _____

   _____

   _____

4. Who is the only one that does not make mistakes?

   _____

5. What is the only true authority?

   _____

6. Sin starts as a

   _____

   _____

7. The church is being led down the garden path of

   _____

   _____

8. God's Word tells us to touch not

   _____

   _____

9. The time will come when people will not endure

   _____

   _____

10. When people refuse to believe the truth, they will be turned to

    _____

    _____

Verse 9

Jude 1:9

Yet Michael the archangel, when contending with the devil he disputed about the body of Moses, durst not bring against him a railing accusation, but said, The Lord rebuke thee.

Bible scholars of the past (the good ones) and of today are at a loss as to exactly what Jude is referring to when he speaks of the "*body of Moses.*" Today **there are no books that bear reference to this event having ever taken place.** Origen mentions such a book, called *The Assumption of Moses,* existing in his time, containing this very account of the contest between Michael and the devil over the body of Moses. Origen supposed that this Jewish-Greek book was the source of Jude's statement. This book is now lost. There is no one to say whether this book existed in Jude's day or not, but **Jude thought this passage was important enough to**

include it in his epistle to the churches.

Do I believe this account ever happened? **If it's included in God's Word, then I believe that it happened, because God's Word is the final authority.** Why, then, would the devil contend with Michael over the body of Moses? To quote Matthew Henry: "Some think that the devil contended that Moses might have a public and honorable funeral, that the place where he was interred might be generally known, hoping thereby to draw the Jews, so naturally prone there to, to a new and fresh instance of idolatry." Jude further tells us that Michael, the archangel of God, would not bring railing arguments against Satan, which is most likely what Satan wanted, but instead, **using the authority given by God, said:** *"The Lord rebuke thee."* The end, the contention, was over; for **God always has the final say.**

When we talk to those in the world, remember, it's fine to discuss the Word, but **when contentions arise, it's time to stop.** When the world comes at me and tells me to prove that God is real, my answer to them is: "You prove to me that God isn't real." So far, **no one has been able to prove to me that God is not real.**

One writer I read said that "the point is that Michael did not rebuke Satan, but left that to the Lord. It is a dangerous thing for God's people to confront Satan directly and to argue with him, because he is much stronger than we are. If an archangel is careful about the way he deals with the devil, how much more cautious ought we to be. While it is true that we share in the victory of Christ, it is also true that we must not be presumptuous. Satan is a dangerous enemy, and when we resist him, we must be sober and vigilant." I know that

Michael is the archangel of God; he is one of the best. But I contend that **we are the born-again believers in the Lord.** As born-again believers, **the spirit of Christ dwells within our hearts.** We have been **washed in the blood of the Lamb,** and we have **power with and through Jesus Christ our Lord.**

Luke 10:17-20

> *[17] And the seventy returned again with joy, saying, Lord, even the devils are subject unto us through thy name.*
> *[18] And he said unto them, I beheld Satan as lightning fall from heaven.*
> *[19] Behold, I give unto you power to tread on serpents and scorpions, and over all the power of the enemy: and nothing shall by any means hurt you.*
> *[20] Notwithstanding in this rejoice not, that the spirits are subject unto you; but rather rejoice, because your names are written in heaven.*

As I read this scripture, it tells me **that we have power over all the powers of the enemy.** Church, rejoice, take a stand, stand up for Jesus and our God and stand up for the one who freed us from Sin. Let us take our rightful place as the children of God. **Let's take the authority given to us by Christ our Lord, bind the forces of the enemy and proclaim healing to the sick, salvation to the lost and freedom to those that are bound.**

Matthew 16:19

And I will give unto thee the keys of the kingdom of heaven: and whatsoever thou shalt bind on earth shall be bound in heaven: and whatsoever thou shalt loose on earth shall be loosed in heaven.

Matthew 18:18

Verily I say unto you, Whatsoever ye shall bind on earth shall be bound in heaven: and whatsoever ye shall loose on earth shall be loosed in heaven.

Review Questions
for Verse 9

1. Who did Michael dispute with?

   _____

   _____

2. What did they dispute over?

   _____

   _____

3. Why did they dispute over this?

   _____

   _____

4. What was Michael's answer to Satan?

   _____

   _____

   _____

5. Origen mentions a book called

   _____

   _____

6. Do you believe this really happened? Why do you believe this?

   _____

   _____

   _____

7. It's fine to discuss the Word of God, but when contention starts, what are we to do?

   _____

   _____

8. Should we come against the devil and what he is doing?

   YES _____   NO _____

9. What makes us different from the angels?

   _____

   _____

10. Jesus gives us power over all of the

    _____

    _____

Verse 10

Jude 1:10

But these speak evil of those things which they know not: but what they know naturally, as brute beasts, in those things they corrupt themselves.

In this verse, Jude continues to warn against false teachers and against listening to false doctrines that are being taught by men and women who do not know the truth or **have changed the truth to suit their own goals and purposes.** But like a lot of people in the world, and particularly in the church, they speak evil of what they do not know. If you want to really make these people angry, try to correct them when they make a mistake or when they try to teach something they know nothing about. As far as these people are concerned, the best way to handle what they don't know is to speak evil of it; to talk bad about any subject that they aren't familiar with, thus setting aside any debate, so their ignorance isn't revealed. Of the things they do know, such as lust, evil passions and sensual pleasure, they run after these, like the animals around us who do what's natural to them. These false teachers corrupt themselves with evil and looking for things to please themselves that are even more evil; for **evil can only be satisfied with things that are worse and worse**, until the devil comes to collect his due.

2 Peter 2:12-14

> *[12] But these, as natural brute beasts, made to be taken and destroyed, speak evil of the things that they understand not; and shall utterly perish in their own corruption;*
> *[13] And shall receive the reward of unrighteousness, as they that count it pleasure to riot in the day time. Spots they are and blemishes, sporting themselves with their own deceivings while they feast with you;*
> *[14] Having eyes full of adultery, and that cannot cease from sin; beguiling unstable souls: an heart they have exercised with covetous practices; cursed children:*

Here is another reference to brute beasts, speaking evil of things that they don't understand, how that they shall perish in their own corruption, that they are going to receive their just rewards. In Revelation, God's Word tells us that **God keeps a record of everything we do or say**, and that we will be judged out of these record books, that **nothing is**

hidden from God. There is, make no doubt about it, a judgment day coming for me and for you. Let us prepare for it now while we still have the time, for the night cometh when no man can work. So **let us work while it is day.**

Review Questions
for Verse 10

1. How do most false teachers try to handle subjects they know nothing about?

   _____

   _____

   _____

2. Evil can only be satisfied with what?

   _____

   _____

   _____

3. What does God's Word tell us that God keeps?

   _____

   _____

   _____

4. How will we be judged?

   _____

   _____

Verse 11

Jude 1:11

Woe unto them! for they have gone in the way of Cain, and ran greedily after the error of Balaam for reward, and perished in the gainsaying of Core.

Jude again speaks dire warnings to the false preachers and teachers, who, as scripture states: *"And through covetousness shall they with feigned words make merchandise of you: whose judgment now of a long time lingereth not, and their damnation slumbereth not."* (2 Peter 2:3) Their only aim is to make merchandise of the flock of God. **They seek to use God's people for their own perverted ends.** Peter's warning mirrors Jude's. I don't know which book was written first, since they were both written in the same year, AD 66. Jude declares, *"Woe unto them,"* then again brings to their and our attention three more examples which we will look at more closely.

First, they have gone in the way of Cain.

Genesis 4:1-15

^{1} And Adam knew Eve his wife; and she conceived, and bare Cain, and said, I have gotten a man from the LORD.
^{2} And she again bare his brother Abel. And Abel was a keeper of sheep, but Cain was a tiller of the ground.
^{3} And in process of time it came to pass, that Cain brought of the fruit of the ground an offering unto the LORD.
^{4} And Abel, he also brought of the firstlings of his flock and of the fat thereof. And the LORD had respect unto Abel and to his offering:
^{5} But unto Cain and to his offering he had not respect. And Cain was very wroth, and his countenance fell.
^{6} And the LORD said unto Cain, Why art thou wroth? and why is thy countenance fallen?
^{7} If thou doest well, shalt thou not be accepted? and if thou doest not well, sin lieth at the door. And unto thee shall be his desire, and thou shalt rule over him.
^{8} And Cain talked with Abel his brother: and it came to pass, when they were in the field, that Cain rose up against Abel his brother, and slew him.
^{9} And the LORD said unto Cain, Where is Abel thy brother? And he said, I know not: Am I my brother's keeper?
^{10} And he said, What hast thou done? the voice of thy brother's blood crieth unto me from the ground.
^{11} And now art thou cursed from the earth, which

hath opened her mouth to receive thy brother's blood from thy hand;

[12] When thou tillest the ground, it shall not henceforth yield unto thee her strength; a fugitive and a vagabond shalt thou be in the earth.

[13] And Cain said unto the LORD, My punishment is greater than I can bear.

[14] Behold, thou hast driven me out this day from the face of the earth; and from thy face shall I be hid; and I shall be a fugitive and a vagabond in the earth; and it shall come to pass, that every one that findeth me shall slay me.

[15] And the LORD said unto him, Therefore whosoever slayeth Cain, vengeance shall be taken on him sevenfold. And the LORD set a mark upon Cain, lest any finding him should kill him.

The story of Cain is a story of pride, anger, hatred, murder and punishment. What do we know about Cain? He was the son of Adam and Eve. We assume that Cain was their firstborn, and Abel was their second son. After the story of Cain and Abel, we are told of the birth of Seth. How many children did Adam and Eve have? No one knows. We do know that when Seth was born, Adam was one hundred thirty years old. After the birth of Seth, Adam lived eight hundred years and begat sons and daughters. How many children could Adam have fathered in eight hundred years? No one knows, but we would venture to say a great number. I was asked one time where Cain got his wife. When I told them that he married his sister, there was a look of shock that came upon their face. If only two people were created, Adam and Eve, then in the beginning, brothers had to marry their sisters. Even Abraham married his half-sister Sarah; they had different mothers but the same father, Terah. *And yet indeed she is my sister; she is the daughter of my father, but not the daughter of my mother; and she became my wife.* (Genesis 20:12)

Now getting back to Cain and his sin, scripture states that there came a time when Cain and Abel brought offerings to present to God. Cain was a farmer, and Abel was a keeper of sheep. When the offerings were laid before the Lord, the Lord accepted Abel's offering but rejected Cain's. Why? Because **there is no remission of sin without the shedding of blood.**

Hebrews 9:22

And almost all things are by the law purged with blood; and without shedding of blood is no remission.

When Adam and Eve sinned and were in disfavor with God, the first thing God did was to make them clothes out of animal skins. When God killed the animals, there was blood shed. **God punished them by casting them out of the garden, but he still had communication and fellowship with man**; look at Enoch who walked with God.

Cain was exceedingly mad because his offering was rejected. I've heard people ask why God didn't accept Cain's offering. He probably brought the best of the things that he had grown, which may have been so. It's believed that even at that time, the people were aware that there needed to be the shedding of blood for a sacrifice. **Cain, in rebellion against God, being disobedient, brought of the fruit of the ground, which God rejected.** Cain became very angry. God then asked Cain why he was angry.

Then, in the seventh verse, God said: *"If thou doest well, shalt thou not be accepted? And if thou doest not well, sin lieth at the door."* God was putting the blame right where it belonged. Cain knew what to do but decided to do things his own way. **When he was rejected, he blamed his brother, and in a fit of rage, killed Able.**

What Jude is saying is that the people were being just like Cain. They were acting in disobedience and rebellion, as Cain had. **Their pride, corruption, and wicked desires were causing them to imitate Cain.**

Second, they ran greedily after the error of Balaam for reward. There are many, many souls who begin in the spirit, but because of events that happen in their lives, they end in the flesh seeking after lustful, damning desires that are impossible to be satisfied. What do we know about Balaam? **Balaam was a prophet of the most high God.** He was a Gentile prophet who tried to curse the Jews. Balak the Moabite king was afraid of the Jews.

Here was a people who had come out of Egypt conquering everything that was in front of them. Balaam was told by God to leave the Jews alone, but he was promised wealth and honor by Balak. **The problem with Balaam is the same that many Christians have today, a covetous heart.** There's nothing wrong with being rich or holding a place of honor, as long as it doesn't interfere with our walk with God. Balaam knew that God had already told him to leave the Jews alone, but **Balaam wanted the money and**

honor that the king promised.

How many people today do we know, or know about, that have traded their Christian principles and values for wealth and fame? **How many preachers have left the preaching of the true Word of God** to become beggars for money, even **trying to "sell" the blessings of God?** (Send me an offering, send me your tithes, and support my ministry.)

These kinds of men and women always speak of "I," look what I have done. What about what God has done? The Bible says except the Lord build the house, they labor in vain that build it. *"Except the LORD build the house, they labour in vain that build it: except the LORD keep the city, the watchman waketh but in vain."* (Psalm 127:1) To boast of self and what I have done is to take the Lord's glory. **The Lord takes a very dim view of those who praise the creature more than the creator.**

Balaam, as we know, was not allowed to curse the Jews. For God to fully get Balaam's attention, God had to speak through the mouth of the ass. **What Balaam intended for a curse, God turned into a blessing.** Looking further at Balaam, we see how Balaam told Balak how to defeat the Jews. Moab was to become friendly with the Jews, invite the Jews to their pagan feasts and mix with the Jews, which is what they did.

Numbers 25:1-9

> *¹ And Israel abode in Shittim, and the people began to commit whoredom with the daughters of Moab.*
> *² And they called the people unto the sacrifices of*

their gods: and the people did eat, and bowed down to their gods.

³ And Israel joined himself unto Baalpeor: and the anger of the LORD was kindled against Israel.

⁴ And the LORD said unto Moses, Take all the heads of the people, and hang them up before the LORD against the sun, that the fierce anger of the LORD may be turned away from Israel.

⁵ And Moses said unto the judges of Israel, Slay ye every one his men that were joined unto Baalpeor.

⁶ And, behold, one of the children of Israel came and brought unto his brethren a Midianitish woman in the sight of Moses, and in the sight of all the congregation of the children of Israel, who were weeping before the door of the tabernacle of the congregation.

⁷ And when Phinehas, the son of Eleazar, the son of Aaron the priest, saw it, he rose up from among the congregation, and took a javelin in his hand;

⁸ And he went after the man of Israel into the tent, and thrust both of them through, the man of Israel, and the woman through her belly. So the plague was stayed from the children of Israel.

⁹ And those that died in the plague were twenty and four thousand.

God's anger was kindled against those who mixed with the Moabites, and twenty and four thousand died. Money does strange things to people who are trying to live right. In an adult Sunday school class, we were talking about tithing. I asked one person if he made a hundred dollars, would he give ten percent, or ten dollars, to the Lord. The answer was, yes. Then I asked, suppose you won the lottery and it was ten million dollars, would you give one million dollars to the church in tithes, which is still ten percent? The person studied for a minute then said, I don't know; one million dollars is a whole lot of money. The percentage is still the same ten percent, but somewhere the dollar amount took over the person's mind. It was no longer a percentage, it became dollars. **Guard yourselves against the tricks of the devil.**

Third, *"And perished in the gainsaying of Core."* As we study out this part of the eleventh verse, we see that Core refers to the Old Testament account of Korah. Korah, like Satan, let jealousy separate him from God. Being vain, he desired the position of Moses. The difference was **Moses was called of God, while Korah was called of self.** It never fails; someone in the church can always run things better than the man of God. He can do things better, he dresses better, and it makes no difference that the pastor is paid three hundred dollars a week, and the complainer makes one thousand dollars a week. The **complainers don't pay their tithes but only give what they think the church needs.** I've seen and heard this for myself. Years ago, in the early 80s, I had a good job making five hundred per week. One day I was talking to one of the men who worked there, and we got onto the subject of churches and tithing. He could not believe that I gave the full ten percent in tithes; this man was a deacon in his church. I asked him, if he didn't tithe, then how much did he give to his church, and his response was ten to fifteen dollars per week, whatever he thought they needed. This man made more per week than I did.

Now, back to Korah. Korah gathered his backers and confronted Moses. Moses told Korah what to do before God, and then on the morrow, God would give the answer. These two hundred fifty men, their wives and children were swallowed up by the ground. **Korah and his followers were priests, but they walked out of God's will and died.** The next day, the people murmured against Moses and Aaron, and God sent a plague among the people, and another fourteen thousand seven hundred died. What Korah started was not limited to Korah and his followers. What he started caused the deaths of the others. **Be careful what you do, because it doesn't just affect you, but others around you.** Don't be a follower of Korah (Core).

Review Questions
for Verse 11

1. When was the Book of Jude believed to have been written?

   _____

   _____

2. How many examples are given in this verse?

   _____

   _____

3. Who is the first example about?

   _____

   _____

   _____

4. How old was Adam when Seth was born?

   _____

5. Abraham was what kin to his wife Sarah?

   _____

   _____

6. There is no remission of sin without what?

   _____

   _____

7. Besides being a prophet of God, what else was Balaam?

   _____

   _____

8. How did God get Balaam's attention?

   _____

   _____

9. Korah desired whose position?

   _____

   _____

10. How many died of the plague?

    _____

    _____

Verses 12-13

Jude 1:12-13

^{12} These are spots in your feasts of charity, when they feast with you, feeding themselves without fear: clouds they are without water, carried about of winds; trees whose fruit withereth, without fruit, twice dead, plucked up by the roots; ^{13} Raging waves of the sea, foaming out their own shame; wandering stars, to whom is reserved the blackness of darkness for ever.

These are spots in your feasts of charity. Now let us ask ourselves a question. What does Jude mean when he refers to these people as spots? *"And shall receive the reward of unrighteousness, as they that count it pleasure to riot in the day time. Spots they are and blemishes, sporting themselves with their own deceivings while they feast with you;"* (2 Peter 2:13) Here Peter refers to these people as spots and blemishes. A spot or blemish is a distraction, something that causes you to look at the spot and not the individual. Have you ever seen a person with a birthmark or scar on their face? In all reality, it's hard not to look or stare at the mark on that person's face. Another thought is that spot means a rock or reef that is sunken under the surface of the water. Then, as boats come into shore, if they are not very careful, the rock or reef will tear into the hull of the boat, thus sinking the vessel. There are many out there today who would dearly love to sink your Christian experience; **to pervert you to their ways of thinking and living.** As Christians bind together for strength, so do those who would pervert the truth. If for some reason we miss heaven because of believing a perverted gospel, when we stand before God, we can blame the false teachers and preachers and be right in doing so, because we were lied to. That, however true, will not excuse us, because we have the written Word, and scripture behooves us to study to show ourselves approved unto God. **No matter how much we seek to justify ourselves and blame others, the accountability still lies squarely upon our shoulders. We make the decisions as to what we believe and accept.**

Jude also speaks of these ungodly souls as *"clouds they are without water, carried about of winds; trees whose fruit withereth, without fruit, twice dead, plucked up by the roots."* It's beautiful to see white billowy clouds in the sky, but as pretty as they are, they carry no rain (water) to give the dry ground. They do nothing to relieve the dry parched ground. **Many so-called Christians are like these clouds, pretty on the outside, but they don't possess the true spirit of God on the inside.** They fill up the pews but do nothing to promote the kingdom of our Lord Jesus Christ.

The second example is of a tree whose fruit is withering away, in the process of backsliding from God. Then to these, Jude adds those without fruit, those who have completely walked away from God for their own selfish desires. **These still profess to be Christians, but they are empty of God's love and grace.** Then Jude makes the statement, *"twice dead."* These words say so much about these individuals. To be twice dead means that at one time they were alive. But you say how can a person be twice dead? It's impossible to live and die twice in the natural world, unless God has performed a miracle. In the spiritual, which Jude is speaking of, it's quite possible. You see, before we came into contact with God's saving grace, we were spiritually dead. As we repented and asked God to save us, we were born again; the old man of sin died. And as scripture states, behold, all things became new. We became a new creature in and through Christ Jesus. As long as we pray and study God's Word and live by the Word, we continue to live a spiritual life, by the power of God. **The moment we decide to walk away from the blessings and grace of God, we die spiritually.** Know this that no man backslides overnight. **If we backslide, it's because we stop praying, studying and seeking the paths of God.** Backsliding is a gradual process of neglecting the things of God.

A perfect example is the prodigal son; we all know of the story of how the younger son asked for his part of the inheritance, which the father gave him. He left the presence of the father. Here is where the son spiritually died. Many will tell you that the son was always a member of the family, and in the natural, he was. But we are talking about the spiritual.

Luke 15:24

For this my son was dead, and is alive again; he was lost, and is found. And they began to be merry.

What does the father say in Luke 15:24? *"For this my son was dead, and is alive again; he was lost, and is found."* **When we choose to walk away from God, we die to the saving grace of God; our names are blotted out of the book of life. We are spiritually dead.**

Revelation 3:5

He that overcometh, the same shall be clothed in white raiment; and I will not blot out his name out of the book of life, but I will confess his name before my Father, and before his angels.

2 Peter 2:20-22

[20] For if after they have escaped the pollutions of the world through the knowledge of the Lord and Saviour Jesus Christ, they are again entangled therein, and overcome, the latter end is worse with them than the beginning.
[21] For it had been better for them not to have known the way of righteousness, than, after they have known it, to turn from the holy commandment delivered unto

them.

²² But it is happened unto them according to the true proverb, The dog is turned to his own vomit again; and the sow that was washed to her wallowing in the mire.

Salvation is the lifeline between us and God. When we allow the devil to break that lifeline, we die in our spirit. Peter says that it is better never to have known the ways of righteousness than to have known it and then turn away. How much plainer can it be said?

Verse 13 talks of the raging waves of the sea, foaming out their own shame, and wandering stars. What punishment do these people deserve? What is their final reward? Jude gives us the answer: *"to whom is reserved the blackness of darkness for ever,"* to be cast into outer darkness forever and ever and ever. To quote Matthew Henry, I give the following: "As for the blackness of darkness for ever, I shall only say that this terrible expression with all the horror it imports, belongs to false teachers, truly, not slanderously so called, who corrupt the Word of God, and betray the souls of men. If this will not make both ministers and people cautious, I know not what will." **How does your life measure up to God's standards?**

To whom are you listening? What are they saying? Remember, many **false preachers and teachers are out to deceive you.** They are changing the Word of God to suit themselves. It's a shame when men and women have decided that they know more than God's prophets and apostles and take the liberty to proclaim themselves wiser and smarter than God's anointed and even wiser than God. They proclaim that the Bible is full of errors and mistakes, and that they know the truth. They are quick to tell you that if you will believe them, they will lead you to a new awaking. Just **remember that when the blind lead the blind, they will both fall into the ditch together.** Be careful whom you listen to and follow, because God keeps a record that we will one day face.

Review Questions
for Verses 12-13

1. II Peter refers to these people as

   _____

   _____

2. Why should we study God's Word?

   _____

   _____

   _____

3. Backsliding is a gradual process of what?

   _____

   _____

   _____

4. When we walk away from God's saving grace, what happens to us?

   _____

   _____

   _____

5. Peter states that it is better never to have known the ways of righteousness than to have known it and

_____

_____

_____

_____

6. What punishment does Jude say these people will receive?

_____

_____

_____

Verses 14-16

Jude 1:14-16

¹⁴ And Enoch also, the seventh from Adam, prophesied of these, saying, Behold, the Lord cometh with ten thousands of his saints, ¹⁵ To execute judgment upon all, and to convince all that are ungodly among them of all their ungodly deeds which they have ungodly committed, and of all their hard speeches which ungodly sinners have spoken against him. ¹⁶ These are murmurers, complainers, walking after their own lusts; and their mouth speaketh great swelling words, having men's persons in admiration because of advantage.

Jude, in this 14th verse, tells us about Enoch and quotes from the *Book of Enoch*, which is several books in one. This quote comes from Book 1, Chapter 1, Verse 9 and reads: "*And behold! He cometh with ten thousands of His holy ones to execute judgement upon all, and to destroy all the ungodly: and to convict all flesh of all the works of their ungodliness which they have ungodly committed, and of all the hard things which ungodly sinners have spoken against Him."*

Jude warns these pretenders that God is not to be played with, neither is His Word; that there is a judgment day coming; and the record books of Heaven hold all the deeds that are not forgiven, all the words spoken against God. Jude goes on to call these ungodly people murmurers and complainers, people walking after their own lusts, and that they speak swelling words. Today we would say flowering words to attract the foolish souls of the unwise; desiring the admiration and acclaim of those around them to build up themselves for their own advantage.

Ecclesiastes 1:9-10

> *⁹ The thing that hath been, it is that which shall be; and that which is done is that which shall be done: and there is no new thing under the sun.*
> *¹⁰ Is there any thing whereof it may be said, See, this is new? it hath been already of old time, which was before us.*

As we study scripture we note over and over that **people everywhere are the same.** The Old Testament through the New Testament teaches us this. As we see in Ecclesiastes 1:9-10, Solomon said that *"there is no new thing under the sun."* How true this is. So shall it be until the final end comes.

The murmurers and complainers are about the same. In *Barnes' Notes on The New Testament,* we quote: "Nothing is more common than for men to complain of their lot; to think that it is hard; to compare theirs with that of others, and to blame God for not having made their circumstances different. The poor complain that they are not rich like others; the sick that they are not well; the enslaved that they are not free; the bereaved that they are deprived of friends; the ugly that they are not beautiful; those in humble life that their lot was not cast among the great and the gay. The virtue that is opposed to this is *contentment*-a virtue of inestimable value." **The ungodly will always work their schemes and will always try to lead God's saints into sin, into compromising their standards.** These ungodly people, as scripture states: *"Having a form of godliness, but denying the power thereof: from such turn away."* (2 Timothy 3:5) What more can I add to this?

Review Questions
for Verses 14 - 16

1. What book does Jude quote from?

   _____

   _____

2. What did King Solomon say?

   _____

   _____

   _____

3. What are we supposed to do about those who only have a form of godliness?

   _____

   _____

   _____

4. People everywhere are what?

   _____

   _____

   _____

5. Nothing is more common for men to do than

   _____

   _____

   _____

Verses 17-19

Jude 1:17-19

^{17} But, beloved, remember ye the words which were spoken before of the apostles of our Lord Jesus Christ; ^{18} How that they told you there should be mockers in the last time, who should walk after their own ungodly lusts. ^{19} These be they who separate themselves, sensual, having not the Spirit.

    We put these three verses together, like we did the verses just before, because they complete a single thought or idea. All through this book, Jude has warned over and over about the results of sin; **he has given example after example from God's Word, whether we like it or not.** That old saying comes to mind: *Turn or Burn*, and speaks volumes of truth. **We and only we are accountable for our own actions.** No one can make us sin against God; we do it because we desire to. The serpent in the garden couldn't make Eve sin; **he tempted her, but the final choice was hers and hers alone.** Adam was the same way; he wasn't forced to eat; he did it because he made the choice to, then tried to put all the blame on Eve for what he chose to do. But **our God was not taken in by Adam's excuse.** They both sinned; the punishment was the same for both, to be cast out of God's perfect garden, to have to make a living by their own hands. **No longer was everything given to them.** Oh, what people throw away when the decision is made to walk away from the love and care of the Savior, the one who died for us so that we might live with Him forever in the Kingdom of Heaven.

Verse 17 tells us to *"remember ye the words which were spoken before of the apostles of our Lord Jesus Christ."* We must remember that at this time in the history of the church, there was no written Bible as we have now. **Today we have the written Word to study and live by, but if we don't remember what it says, there's no way we can live a Christian life.** Many people think that going to church is serving God; they go once a week, and that's enough. What I maintain is that we don't go to church to serve God. **We go to church to learn how to serve God**, that going to church teaches us and brings to our remembrance the things we already know. **We need a continual renewing of God's Word in our lives.**

Romans 15:4

> *For whatsoever things were written aforetime were written for our learning, that we through patience and comfort of the scriptures might have hope.*

Romans 15:4 states that we are to learn God's Word, for by the Word we gain contentment and hope in our souls. **The peace of God quiets the troubled soul**, while the 18th verse speaks of mockers in the last days walking after the lust of their souls. Sadly, we are living in the days Jude was speaking about, the last days; they are here**. Now is the time to search our souls.**

Review Questions
for Verses 17 - 19

1. Why are these three verses put together?

   _____

   _____

   _____

2. Who is accountable for our actions?

   _____

   _____

   _____

3. Can Satan make us sin?

   _____

   _____

   _____

4. Verse 17 tells us to remember what?

   _____

   _____

   _____

5. Why do we go to church?

   _____

   _____

   _____

6. What do we gain by learning God's Word?

   _____

   _____

   _____

Verses 20-21

Jude 1:20-21

^{20} But ye, beloved, building up yourselves on your most holy faith, praying in the Holy Ghost, ^{21} Keep yourselves in the love of God, looking for the mercy of our Lord Jesus Christ unto eternal life.

"Building up yourselves on your most holy faith, praying in the Holy Ghost." The Word here is trying to get the Christian to realize **that we must have a daily walk with the Lord.** Our most holy faith is the same faith that was once delivered to the saints, the faith we received at salvation. Once received, **it becomes our duty to add to this faith, by studying, praying and living according to thus saith the Lord.** We are called upon by the Word to live so that a lost and dying world may see the power and joy of God within us and seek what we have. The Christian must realize that his life, actions, and character are the only Bible that most

sinners ever read.

The sinner watches our lives. He or she may not go to church but still knows right from wrong. I've heard many a sinner say, "Well, so and so can't be a Christian, because they do the same things that I do." **We are being watched and judged by our actions.** I, as well as you, know people who drink, get drunk, cuss, take the Lord's name in vain, lie, cheat, steal, and go to church and claim to be a Christian. There is no way, according to scripture, that this is possible.

Praying in the Holy Ghost, what does this mean? To the Pentecostal Christian, it means praying until you get into the spirit of prayer, praying in tongues, and praying with groanings that cannot be uttered.

Romans 8:26-27

> *26 Likewise the Spirit also helpeth our infirmities: for we know not what we should pray for as we ought: but the Spirit itself maketh intercession for us with groanings which cannot be uttered.*
> *27 And he that searcheth the hearts knoweth what is the mind of the Spirit, because he maketh intercession for the saints according to the will of God.*

To the people who are not Pentecostal but true saints of God, it's the same without the speaking or praying in tongues. **One of the greatest problems in the Christian movement today is denominationalism**, or a better way to put it is separatism, which is not crossing denominational boundaries. **Denominations won't take us to Heaven**, for **only the shed blood of Jesus Christ can do that.**

Pentecostal or not, **pray until you get in the spirit of prayer, that special place where your soul communes with the Lord.** Finally, keep yourselves in the love of God and His mercy until **Jesus our Lord comes back for His church (all born-again believers).**

The key to serving God and living for him is to keep yourself from worldly living, which prospers nothing but to condemn our souls before God. I know that to **live for God**, to **hold godly standards**, brings criticism from the world. They call us names; they make jokes about us; but isn't seeing our Lord in heaven worth it all?

We never give up anything for God, except he repays our sacrifice with something far better than we gave up. **We cannot afford to get materialistic with God.** If you serve God for what you can get out of it, then you serve God for the wrong reason. In this world where many are trying to use God for their own desire, they have a rude awakening coming. **Be not deceived**, for **God is not mocked**, for **whatsoever a man soweth, that shall he also reap.**

Review Questions
for Verses 20 - 21

1. We are to build up ourselves on our most

   _____

   _____

2. Christians must realize that we must

   _____

   _____

   _____

3. Christians must realize that their lives are the only

   _____

   _____

   _____

4. What does scripture mean when it speaks of praying in the Holy Ghost?

   _____

   _____

   _____

5. What is one of the greatest problems in the Christian movement?

   _____

   _____

   _____

6. What is the only thing that can take us to heaven?

   _____

   _____

   _____

7. The key to serving God and living for him is to

   _____

   _____

   _____

Verses 22-25

Jude 1:22-25

²² And of some have compassion, making a difference: ²³ And others save with fear, pulling them out of the fire; hating even the garment spotted by the flesh. ²⁴ Now unto him that is able to keep you from falling, and to present you faultless before the presence of his glory with exceeding joy, ²⁵ To the only wise God our Saviour, be glory and majesty, dominion and power, both now and ever. Amen.

Verse 22 begins with, *"And of some have compassion, making a difference."* Does this mean that we are to only try to reach certain people? No, **it tells us that there are differences in people and how we are to approach them.** Who then are those to whom we are to have compassion? These are the ones who have a good heart but have erred from the pure truth of the Word. They can also be those who have been hurt in church and have backed off from really getting in and serving God. **It's a shame that we as Christians are sometimes so thoughtless that we speak before we think about what we're saying and hurt our brothers and sisters in Christ.**

We must remember **we aren't judges**; the Lord does all the judging. We are to have a Christ-like spirit and approach these people with love and tenderness. **We must be Christ's hand extended**, a hand of compassion making a difference in the lives of people.

"And others save with fear, pulling them out of the fire;" We are to save with fear, urging upon them the results of a life of sin. Matthew Henry says, "Endeavour to frighten them out of their sins; preach hell and damnation to them." Always **using care and caution not to drive them away**, we must be led by the spirit of God, **letting God open up the doors of their heart.** Too many times we have a problem distinguishing between the sinner and the sin. They are two different things. Too many times we see only the sin, overlooking the sinner caught in the devil's snare. This is why we must always stress to above all, **love the sinner, while at the same time hating the sin**; remembering that except for the grace of God, there go we.

In these last two verses, Jude stresses the fact that if we will hold onto God, that He will be the force that will keep us from falling. He (God) will at that day, when we come before Him, present us faultless before His glory with exceeding joy as it states in the 24th verse: *"Now unto him that is able to keep you from falling, and to present you faultless before the presence of his glory with exceeding joy."* (Jude 1:24)

The closing verse sums up the glory of God by saying, *"To the only wise God our Saviour, be glory and majesty, dominion and power, both now and ever. Amen."*

Review Questions
for Verses 22 - 25

1. *And on some have compassion making a difference* tells us what?

   _____

   _____

2. Who then are those on whom we are to have compassion?

   _____

   _____

   _____

3. As Christians we must remember that we are not judges, but that

   _____

   _____

4. One of the biggest problems with Christians is that they

   _____

   _____

5. What does Matthew Henry say of those we are to pull out of the fire?

　

　

　

6. When dealing with the lost, we too many times have a problem. What is it?

Bibliography

I would like to give my sincere thanks to the following writers who helped make this bible study on *A Study of the Warnings of Jude* possible. These writers have given me so much insight and knowledge. These authors were truly used of God; most have already gone home to be with the Lord. I can only say of them, that they left a wealth of knowledge behind. Now we as ministers and teachers need to use it, to build and strengthen the church of our precious Lord Jesus Christ. Thank you.

Brother Wilson

Rev. Frank Thompson D.D., Ph.D.
    Thompson Chain Reference Bible KJV
    B. B. Kirkbride Bible Co. Inc.
    Indianapolis, Indiana
    63rd printing
    Copyright 1964

Rev. Matthew Henry
    Matthew Henry's Commentary on the Whole Bible
    Hendrickson Publishers Inc.
    Fifth printing – May 1998
    Copyright 1991

Rev. Albert Barnes
    Barnes' Notes on the New Testament
    Baker Book House Company
    Grand Rapids, Michigan
    Reprinted 2005

Reprinted from the 1847 edition published by
Blackie & Son, London

Rev. Warren W. Wiersbe
The Wiersbe Bible Commentary: New Testament
Published by David C. Cook
Colorado Springs, Colorado
Second Edition 2007

Rev. Michael Green, M.A., B.D.
Introduction and Commentary on
The Second Epistle of Peter and the Epistle of Jude
Tyndale New Testament Commentaries
Wm. B. Eerdman Publishing Company
Grand Rapids, Michigan
Fourth printing 1977

Rev. Finis Jennings Dake
The Dake Annotated Reference Bible KJV
Dake Bible Sales Inc.
Lawrenceville, Georgia
Twenty-seventh printing – April 1998
Copyright 1963, 1991

Jay P. Green Sr.
General Editor and Translator
The Interlinear Bible
Hebrew, Greek, English
Sovereign Grace Publishers
Second Edition Copyrighted 1986

Flavius Josephus (37 AD – 100 AD)
>   *Josephus the Complete Works*
>   Translated by William Whiston, A.M.
>   Kregel Publications
>   Grand Rapids, Michigan
>   Copyright 1960
>   Fourteenth printing 1977

W. E. Vine, M. A. (1873 – 1949)
Merrill F. Unger, Th.M., Th.D., Ph.D. (1909 – 1980)
William White Jr., Th.M., Ph.D.
>   *Vine's Complete Expository Dictionary of Old and New Testament Words*
>   Thomas Nelson Publishers
>   Nashville, Tennessee
>   Published 1985
>   Copyright 1984

J. D. Douglas, M.A., B.D., S.T.M., Ph.D.
Organizing Editor of
>   *The New Bible Dictionary*
>   Wm. B. Eerdmans Publishing Co.
>   Grand Rapids, Michigan

Rev. Eberhand Nestle
>   *Greek – English New Testament*
>   Greek Text – Literal Interlinear
>   King James Version
>   New International Version
>   Christianity Today
>   Washington, D.C.

Rev. Marvin R. Vincent, D.D.
    Vincent's Word Studies in the New Testament
    Hendrickson Publishers
    Peabody, Maine

Rev. Adam Clarke (1762 – 1832)
    Adam Clarke's Commentary on the Bible
    Abridged by Ralph Earle
    Baker Book House
    Grand Rapids, Michigan
    Copyright 1967
    Tenth printing – August 1977

Webster's New World College Dictionary
    IDG Books Worldwide Inc.
    An International Data Group Company
    Foster City, California
    Fourth Edition
    Copyright 2000

Robert A. Baker and John M. Landers
    Christian History, A Summary of
    B & H Publishing Group
    Nashville, Tennessee
    Copyright 2005

Review Questions Answers

Answers

Review of a Jewel in 25 Verses (page 15)

1. 25
2. A warning
3. Teachings that pervert the true Word of God
4. We are children by adoption when we accept Jesus as our savior
5. A lack of knowledge concerning God's Word
6. To win souls to the Lord

Review of a General Epistle (page 19)

1. A general epistle
2. It is written to all Christians everywhere
3. II Peter
4. Indifference
5. We will fall prey to the devil
6. The enemy will sow tares in our fields or lives
7. Be watchful

Review Questions for Verses 1-2 (page 33)

1. The brother of James, the brother of Jesus Christ
2. Yes – two or more

3. James
4. To them that are sanctified by God the Father and preserved in Jesus Christ and called
5. No we send ourselves there
6. Yes. By giving their lives for the sake of God's kingdom
7. The world
8. The truth will set us free

Review Questions for Verse 3 (page 41)

1. He was troubled by what was happening in the church
2. An attempt to explain the nature of evil, the nature of God and His relation to the world and the present order of existence.
3. The common salvation is the fact that are all saved the same way
4. The church is bending and bowing at the altar of the world
5. Faith
6. Every creature
7. By the preaching of the gospel

Review Questions for Verse 4 (page 51)

1. A warning
2. To destroy the church
3. By our own free will
4. That there is nothing new under the sun

5. No one but us
6. The sinner's sins follow after them to judgment. The saint's sins have gone before them to be forgiven.
7. Saved by grace
8. Great harm by destroying the souls of man

Review Questions for Verse 5 (page 61)

1. Remembrance of things that they already knew
2. By repetition
3. Stir up your pure minds by way of remembrance
4. Israel leaving Egypt
5. Everyone twenty years and up, except for Joshua and Caleb
6. 40 years
7. A way of escape

Review Questions for Verse 6 (page 71)

1. Be in our lives at all
2. That God does and, will hold us accountable for our unbelief, our actions, and our choices we make.
3. Yes. Without a certain amount of free will, how could they rebel against God and go with the devil.
4. Satan, the devil
5. One third of the angels of heaven
6. In hell, in chains of darkness

Review Questions for Verse 7 (page 85)

1. The very appearance of evil
2. Something to be obeyed
3. Total destruction
4. Admah and Zeboim
5. Old things pass away, all things become new
6. They worshiped the creature more than the creator
7. Turns us over to a reprobate mind
8. At the house of God

Review Questions for Verse 8 (page 91)

1. No
2. Delusions
3. Ye shall be as gods
4. God
5. The word of God
6. Tiny spark and grows
7. Apostasy
8. Mine anointed, and do my prophets no harm
9. Sound doctrine
10. Fables

Review Questions for Verse 9 (page 97)

1. The devil
2. The body of Moses
3. No one knows for sure but think that it was over where Moses was to be buried

4. The Lord rebuke thee
5. <u>The Assumption of Moses</u>
6. Yes, Because the Bible says so
7. We are to S T O P
8. Yes
9. We are saved through the shed blood of Jesus Christ
10. All the powers of the enemy

Review Questions for Verse 10 (page 103)

1. To speak evil of it
2. Things that are worse and worse
3. A record of everything we do or say
4. Out of God's record books

Review Questions for Verse 11 (page 115)

1. AD 66
2. Three
3. Cain
4. About 130 years old
5. Brother or half brother
6. The shedding of blood
7. Gentile
8. He spoke to Balaam through the mouth of an ass
9. Moses
10. 24,000 perished

Review Questions for Verses 12-13 (page 123)

1. Spots and blemishes
2. To show ourselves approved unto God
3. Neglecting the things of God
4. We die spiritually
5. Then turn away
6. To whom is reserved the blackness of darkness forever

Review Questions for Verses 14-16 (page 129)

1. The Book of Enoch
2. There is no new thing under the sun
3. From such turn away
4. The same
5. Complain

Review Questions for Verses 17-19 (page 135)

1. They complete a single thought or ideal
2. We and only we are
3. No one but ourselves
4. The word spoken by the Apostles
5. To learn how to serve God
6. Contentment and hope in our souls

Review Questions for Verses 20-21 (page 141)

1. Holy faith

2. Have a daily walk with the Lord
3. Bible that most sinners ever read
4. Pray until we get into the spirit of prayer
5. Denominationalism or separatism
6. The shed blood of Jesus Christ
7. Keep yourselves from worldly living

Review Questions for Verses 22-25 (page 147)

1. That there are difference in people and how we are to reach them
2. These are they who have a good heart, but have erred from the truth of God's Word
3. God does the judging
4. Speak before they think about what they are saying
5. Endeavor to frighten them out of their sin; preach hell and damnation to them
6. Distinguishing between the sinner and the sin

— Notes —

— Notes —

— Notes —

— Notes —

— Notes —

Coming Summer 2018!

Look for Rev. Wilson's upcoming book, ***A Study on 1st and 2nd Peter***, through **Paradise Gospel Press** and **Amazon**. Enjoy the following excerpt from the book:

A Study on First Peter

Chapter One

1 Peter 1:1

Peter, an apostle of Jesus Christ, to the strangers scattered throughout Pontus, Galatia, Cappadocia, Asia, and Bithynia,

In this first verse, Peter tells the readers who he is. He is an apostle of Jesus Christ. What is an apostle? An apostle is a person who had a special and very personal encounter with Jesus. A good definition of an apostle is: One who is sent on a mission by the Lord. Apostles have special power and speak with an authority given by God. I believe there are apostles in the churches today; men who are ordained by God to fill this office in our local assemblies. We know the disciples were witnesses of the resurrected Christ and were called apostles. Paul also had a personal encounter with

Jesus on the road to Damascus. Some say that Paul was the greatest of the apostles, for he surely had a special mission from the Lord, to preach salvation to the Gentiles.

Peter's life of following Jesus must have been glorious. To think that he was witness to the miracles that Jesus preformed: the healing of the sick; the raising of the dead; the feeding the thousands of people with five loaves and two fishes. All these things Peter saw with his own eyes. Peter has his own victories and failures, such as walking on the water to go to Jesus then sinking and crying out to Jesus for help. This was a failure, but victory was still his as he walked back to the ship with Jesus. Then there was the outpouring of the Holy Ghost on the day of Pentecost. Is it any wonder Peter became one of the foundation stones upon which the church was built? Peter, I am sure, was determined to overcome his failure and to rise above his denial of Jesus. This he did with trust and faith in Jesus.

Luke 22:31-34

> *31 And the Lord said, Simon, Simon, behold, Satan hath desired to have you, that he may sift you as wheat:*
> *32 But I have prayed for thee, that thy faith fail not: and when thou art converted, strengthen thy brethren.*
> *33 And he said unto him, Lord, I am ready to go with thee, both into prison, and to death. 34 And he said, I tell thee, Peter, the cock shall not crow this day, before that thou shalt thrice deny that thou knowest me.*

Here in Luke 22, Jesus instructs Peter, after he is converted, to strengthen the brethren. This part of the verse, "when thou are converted," is speaking of Peter after his denial of Christ three times, then going out and bitterly praying and repenting of his failure before God.

John 21:15-17

> *15 So when they had dined, Jesus saith to Simon Peter, Simon, son of Jonas, lovest thou me more than these? He saith unto him, Yea, Lord; thou knowest that I love thee. He saith unto him, Feed my lambs.*
> *16 He saith to him again the second time, Simon, son of Jonas, lovest thou me? He saith unto him, Yea, Lord; thou knowest that I love thee. He saith unto him, Feed my sheep.*
> *17 He saith unto him the third time, Simon, son of Jonas, lovest thou me? Peter was grieved because he said unto him the third time, Lovest thou me? And he said unto him, Lord, thou knowest all things; thou knowest that I love thee. Jesus saith unto him, Feed my sheep.*

In John 21, Jesus asks three times, "Lovest thou me?" Peter replies, "Lord, you know that I love you." The first time Jesus said, "Feed my lambs." The second and third times Jesus said, "Feed my sheep." This was a message of what Peter was to do. After Peter repented of his failures, his life was changed.

He then came back and pulled the other disciples together to encourage them, to be the leader that Jesus intended for him to be. The apostles were the messengers of the gospel, the founders of the Christian church. They were sent out anointed of God. God used them to spread the word of God with signs following. They were filled with the Holy Ghost and spoke with other tongues as the Spirit gave them utterance. They worked miracles through faith in God.

John 14:12-14

> *12 Verily, verily, I say unto you, He that believeth on me, the works that I do shall he do also; and greater works than these shall he do; because I go unto my Father.*
> *13 And whatsoever ye shall ask in my name, that will I do, that the Father may be glorified in the Son.*
> *14 If ye shall ask any thing in my name, I will do it.*

The Word tells us in John 14 that Jesus said, "*He that believeth on me*" shall do great works, greater even than Jesus did; that we, as the born-again children of God, can ask in the name of Jesus for God to move, to heal, to work miracles, to have his will in hearts and lives; and according to the Word of God, Jesus will do it all for the glory of God and His kingdom.

This is what Jesus taught His disciples and the apostles. This same message transitions from the time of Christ through the ages to this present day. The message is just as powerful now as then, and the meaning is the same. We have the right to ask of Christ, believing, standing on our most holy faith, and Jesus is bound by his holy word to meet the need, as long as it brings glory and honor to God the Father.

Did you know that the only unfinished book in the Bible is the book of Acts? Because the acts of the Apostles, all true Christian believers, and the acts of the church are still going on around the world. Just as the church and true believers in Christ were persecuted in the beginning, so are they being persecuted and martyred today. To quote from the book *Encyclopedia of Christian Martyrs:* "Persecution of Christians is more widespread in this century than it was in the time of the Roman Empire, and the church cannot ignore the problem. More than an estimated 160,000 believers were martyred in 1996 alone." An example of this is Graham Staines and his sons, who were burned to death by Hindu extremists in 1999.

Peter knew what manner of death he would face; Jesus told him. Jesus also told him to strengthen the brethren, to preach the word, to lead men and women to the foot of the cross where they would find their hearts' desire: peace in their troubled souls; peace in the time of trouble; peace when the storms of life are raging; peace, perfect peace in Jesus. Who was Peter? He was a steadfast rock, unshakeable, unmovable in Christ Jesus. He was the glue that helped hold the new-found church together. He was the voice of reason, when there was none. He was the voice of rebuke when needed, the voice of hope and encouragement; he was the rock.

As Peter begins this letter, he addresses it to the strangers that were scattered throughout Pontus, Galatia, Cappadocia, Asia, and Bithynia. Peter, as he begins to write, stresses that he is an apostle of Jesus Christ. This means he is called of the Lord and that he speaks for the Lord here on earth. As Peter speaks of strangers, he is not just speaking of displaced people from their homeland; then as today, when we speak of ourselves as pilgrims and strangers, we are confessing that this world is not our home, that our home is in heaven where Jesus, our Lord, has prepared a place for us. We have become sojourners in this world. When we gave our hearts and lives to Jesus our Savior, we became citizens of the kingdom of heaven.

John 14:1-3

> *¹ Let not your heart be troubled: ye believe in God, believe also in me.*
> *² In my Father's house are many mansions: if it were not so, I would have told you. I go to prepare a place for you.*
> *³ And if I go and prepare a place for you, I will come again, and receive you unto myself; that where I am, there ye may be also.*

The Word tells us Jesus has a place prepared for us, that where He is, there we might be also. We, as the blood-bought, redeemed children of God, are the blessed Bride of Christ. To the true believer death is not the end of life; it is just the beginning of life. As one person related to me, death is just exhaling in this world to inhale in the presence of Jesus and God the Father, to live forever. Another example we use is to close our eyes in death here, to open them in the presence of God. No one wants to die, but to the Christian, there is no fear of death; to die is to go home.

www.ingramcontent.com/pod-product-compliance
Lightning Source LLC
LaVergne TN
LVHW051834080426
835512LV00018B/2879